The *How* and the *Tao* of Old Time Banjo

by Patrick Costello

For Tiny.

ISBN 0-9744190-0-1

Pick-Ware Publications
PO Box 110 Crisfield, MD 21817
http://www.pick-ware.com

Contents

Introduction

"What have you got, kid?" The old man asked me around his cigar.

"A banjo!" I replied.

"I know *that* you little dipstick." He said rolling his eyes "You think somebody as old as I am hasn't seen a banjo before? What have you got? Play something."

I thought about trying to say something to get out of this. As I stood there fidgeting the old man shook his head, picked up his guitar and started to walk away.

Oh man, I thought to myself, I'm really blowing something here. It was an August day. The festival was being held on this big open field and the sun was just hammering down on us. I knew a total of three and a half songs. I didn't want to make a fool out of myself but I also had the feeling that if I chickened out here I was going to miss out on something. I closed my eyes for a second, took a deep breath, moved my banjo strap a little bit on my shoulder and started to pound my way through a tune called "The White House Blues".

The old man cocked his head and nodded a little before he turned around. He stood there holding a beat up guitar while cigar smoke billowed around his head. He seemed to enjoy listening to me ruin a perfectly good song.

He didn't walk away and he didn't tell me to stop so I ran through the tune again. I looked back up and saw that the old man had waved a couple of his buddies over. Old guys wearing kaki slacks that went up nearly to their armpits slinging battered guitars and mandolins gathered around me.

"That almost sounds like White House Blues."

"Can't be. Ain't no kid that young knows that song."

"It might be The White House Blues, but the kid is so scared that he's playing it too fast."

Nobody said stop so I ran through it again. I was starting to calm down a bit. The old man with the guitar said something to one of the guys standing around me that I didn't hear but his cronies all got a good chuckle out of it. Most of the time he just listened with his head sort of cocked off to one side while he smoked his cigar and tapped his foot.

I finished another run through the song and stopped. The old guys gave a little cheer and a couple of them gave me a pat on the back saying, "not bad, kid!" The old man with the guitar just went on smoking for a moment. Then he began playing "The White House Blues". A fiddle joined in. Then a mandolin and a few more guitars started weaving in and out of the melody. They ran through that song the way you would walk through your own living room.

In other words, they played it a heck of a lot better than I did.

After playing the song a few times the old guy with the cigar nodded to his buddies and they all ended at the same time. The playing was great but that trick of everybody stopping at the same time just blew me away.

He said, "First thing you've got to do is slow down. Then you want to work on that move into the F chord. You can try it like this." He went on to show me a couple of tricks to smooth out the song while his gang looked on.

One of the other guys showed me a lick and another had me play the song again while he thumped out the rhythm on his mandolin.

"It's the rhythm, kid," he said "That's got to stay the same no matter what happens."

Once they knew that I was getting what they were showing me they sort of backed off and the old guy with the cigar said, "Ok now, get lost. Go on and work on that. Don't come back until you can do like we showed you." And they all walked away leaving me standing in the hot August sun wondering what the heck had just happened.

I did go home and practice what they shared with me and I kept coming back. Not just to that group of old men but anywhere I could run into somebody and pick up a tune, lick or idea.

I am starting out with this story because it is really important that you understand right off the bat that you cannot become a banjo player from reading a book.

I can share with you the basic techniques needed to start playing and I can show you some tricks that will make your playing more exciting but nothing is going to take the place of experience.

I got started on the banjo when I was fifteen years old because my father bet me his banjo that I couldn't teach myself how to play it. Today my father and I like to joke that while he might have lost the bet he came out a winner because the two of us have had some pretty amazing adventures over the years sharing our love of music with people around the world.

As a kid in Philadelphia I found it hard to glean useful information about playing the banjo from books. There were one or two good titles but most of the things I know about the banjo today are either the result of thousands of hours of playing or were taught to me by other banjo players. Back then I used to talk quite a bit about how much easier it would be to learn the banjo if there was a book that just laid out how things worked. A book that said, "Ok now, go on and work on that. Don't come back until you can do like we showed you."

An old banjo-picking friend always said that he was going to write that book. He would ramble on for hours about how he was going to write it all down but he never got around to picking up a pencil. When he passed away a few years ago I figured that book was never going to be published because I sure wasn't going to write it.

Not too long ago a teacher friend of mine mentioned that he was starting an after school banjo program so I decided to put together a couple of pages covering tuning and basic old time banjo skills to get the kids started. It was never my intention to write a "banjo book" but when I got past sixty pages I realized that this was going to be a little bit more than a mimeographed handout. It was turning into something like the resource that we talked about all those years ago.

Don't go into this thinking that you can work your way through it in a weekend. It's going to take a good deal of time and hard work just to get the basic frailing strum down smooth. It's going to take you time to be able to change a few chords without screwing up.

An old friend of mine used to tell his students that it takes about five hundred to a thousand hours of practice to become a half-decent banjo player. Whether those hours take months or years to complete depends on how hard you are willing to work.

The good news is that if all you ever manage to learn is the basic strum and three chords you can play thousands, yes *thousands,* of songs.

I don't expect you to be familiar with all the songs in this book. When I was just starting on the banjo a big part of the fun was the fact that everything was brand new. In a lot of ways not having somebody around to tell me exactly how a song should be played gave me the freedom to come up with my own ideas. Most of these songs are very old but to a beginner they are brand spanking new.

If you do get stuck on the melody line of a song I suggest that you do what I did and go exploring. Find an old guitar player in your town. Bug the local radio station to play some folk music. Browse the Internet or just make something up. There is no right or wrong way here. Just follow your heart.

So take your time with this book. Get a technique or a lick out of it. Then get lost for a while and "Don't come back until you can do like we showed you."

Patrick Costello
Crisfield, Maryland
April, 2003

My father, known to our banjo students around the world as **"Dear Old Dad,"** was instrumental in both helping me learn to play the banjo and putting the book together. I asked him to write down a few thoughts to help get things rolling.

-Patrick

Thoughts from Dear Old Dad

There is a lot of "stuff" in this book. The 5-string banjo is a great deal of fun to play and learn but please remember that the mastery of any instrument is a life long process. Take your time and get the basics down solid. Relax and enjoy the small successes that are the result of practice and hard work. Trust me, there is no easy way. You cannot substitute anything else for "time behind the pot." Remember, the guy who practices the most gets the gigs.

Patrick and I have had a lot of musical adventures. I can remember us sitting in on jam sessions wondering how we would ever be able to play and sing "like that." Well, we worked at it and now folks look at us and say the same thing. The fun is not in the being there. The fun is in the journey. I would not trade the most embarrassing musical moment spent with my son for anything. The memories are priceless and best of all they are mine.

I know that our methods work. All I have to do is watch our "students" play, teach and share music with other people. They all started with the basic frailing strum, a desire to learn and a commitment to progress. You can do it. Keep an open mind. Explore different ideas and sounds. Play anywhere and everywhere that you can. If you wait until you are "good enough" you never will be.

The happiest people that I have met on the musical road are families. Get your kids involved as soon as they show interest and you will have your own adventures to write about some day.

Thank you son. It has not always been easy but we sure had a wild old time.

Pat Costello
May, 2003

The *How* of Old-Time Banjo

If you ask five different banjo players what the term "old-time banjo" means you are likely to get twenty different answers.

Some folks will say that old-time banjo is all about playing fiddle tunes note-for-note right along with a fiddler. Some will tell you that it's all about minor key and modal tunes relating to coal miners and murderers. Other players will say it's about rhythm and another will say that it's all about alternate tunings and historical interpretation.

The funny thing is that they are all right in some way or another.

Old-time banjo takes a little bit from every kind of music that has come into America since the colonial days and mixes it up into an extremely powerful and dynamic approach to music.

Rather than focus on any one aspect of old-time banjo playing I've found that things seem to work better in the beginning if you learn a handful of basic techniques. These can then be used to make the music that *you* want to play. In the following pages we will talk a little bit about banjo setup and proceed to dive into the basic frailing strum. After that things will start to speed up. Near the end of this "How" section you will find tips on reading music and playing by ear. None of these techniques are absolutely required to play the banjo. They are offered here because you may well need them for something you want to do down the road.

Of all the techniques in this book the basic frailing strum is the most important because everything else, from playing and singing to laying down sizzling fast licks in a fiddle tune or a breakdown, is built on the basic strum.

Take your time with the basic strum and get used to playing rhythm and changing chords before you start exploring other techniques. What you do and where you go after the frailing strum is up to you. It's *your* banjo and it's *your* music.

Getting Started

I'm going to take a leap of faith here and assume that you have a five-string banjo.

The basic parts of a banjo are shown on the graphic on this page. I don't want to get too specific about this because there are just too many variations in five-string banjo design to list.

Your banjo may or may not have a resonator (a big dish attached to the back of the banjo) and it may or may not have a tone ring (a metal or wooden hoop under the head that makes the banjo ring.) You may have what's referred to as a mountain banjo or you may be playing a copy of an early minstrel era banjo.

Whatever it is it'll work but if you want to play you are going to have to get it properly set up and in tune.

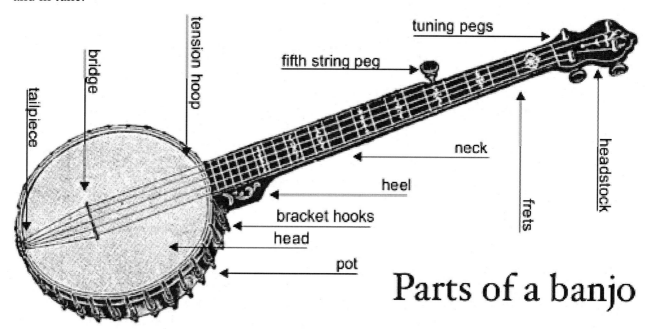

Parts of a banjo

Tuning Your Banjo

Of all the skills required to play the banjo tuning is probably one of the most difficult to master. It is going to take you a while to get used to how your banjo is supposed to sound.

When people refer to the strings of a banjo they are almost always numbered one through five with the fifth string being the short string ending at a peg located at the fifth fret.

I strongly recommend that you purchase an electronic chromatic tuner. It makes learning how to tune much easier.

There are quite a few makes and models on the market with a pretty wide price range. I would not recommend buying the most expensive tuner because if you start playing out you will most likely lose or drop it. I've left more than one nice tuner sitting on a park bench or in a church hall never thinking about it until I was more than halfway home.

When you are tuning your banjo you should know how the strings are numbered. The short string is the fifth string. When you are holding your banjo the fifth string will be on top and the first sting will be closest to the floor.

Your banjo is tuned to an open G chord.

The fifth string is tuned to **G**.
The fourth string is tuned to **D**.
The third string is tuned to **G**.
The second string is tuned to **B**.
The first string is tuned to **D**.

Be sure to have the string ringing when you crank on your tuning pegs. This helps you avoid tightening the string past its' breaking point.

To tune your banjo without a tuner just follow these steps:

1. Assume that your **first** string is at least close to being in tune.

2. Play your **second** string at the **third** fret.
    Tune it up or down so that it matches the sound of the **first** string played open.

3. Play your **third** string at the **fourth** fret.
    Tune it up or down so that it matches the sound of the **second** string played open.

4. Play your **fourth** string at the **fifth** fret.
    Tune it up or down so that it matches the sound of the **third** string played open.

5. The **fifth** string played open should sound the same as the first string played at the **fifth** fret.

This also works as a quick and easy way to check your tuning between songs. Just don't do it into the microphone if you are on stage.

Setting Up Your Banjo

If the bridge is out of place no amount of tuning is going to make your banjo sound right. A quick & easy way to check bridge position is to take an electronic tuner and compare the sound of the first string played both open and fretted at the twelfth fret. Your tuner should give you a D note for both the fretted & open strings. If your first string fretted at the twelfth fret reads a little sharp or flat just move the bridge backward or forward until it's in tune.

Once you get the bridge in the proper position mark around the feet with a pencil so that you can put it back in the correct place easily.

The bridge is held in place by the tension of the strings. If you slacken or remove the strings the bridge will fall off. **Do not glue the bridge in place.**

I really like the way my banjo plays with a low bridge but most new banjos come with a pretty high bridge and action ("action" is a term musicians use to describe how high the strings are from the fretboard) so you may want to visit your local music shop to try out a few different bridges. They are not expensive and there are a lot of different types and heights both standard and compensated.
(A compensated bridge is designed to make the third string intonate properly.) You will be amazed at the difference that bridge height or thickness can make to playability and tone.

On some banjos you can adjust the tension of the strings behind the bridge with the tailpiece. Experiment with it and see what you get. The "trick" to using an adjustable tailpiece is to push the tailpiece down towards the head with one hand to take the pressure off the adjusting screw on the back of the tailpiece. Use your free hand to tighten or loosen the adjusting screw.

Strings

I prefer light gauge strings. I know a lot of folks who think that a banjo needs *really* heavy strings but the problem for a beginner is that heavier strings are harder to play. Believe me, high actions and heavy strings have caused many new banjo players to quit.

Do yourself a favor and start out with light gauge strings and a reasonably low action. There is no need to complicate the learning process by adding cramped and torn up fingers.

On some short-scale banjos a heavier gauge string is needed because with a shorter neck there is a lot more "play" in the strings.

Some banjos were never designed to use steel strings but rather strings made out of nylon or gut. If you plan on starting with an old banjo be certain that it will take the tension of steel strings. If you are not sure always ask!

Your banjo strings run from the tailpiece, over the bridge, over the nut and attach to the tuning pegs in the headstock. The tricky part of stringing your banjo is attaching the strings to the tuning pegs and getting everything in the right direction. The headstock diagram shows how it works. This is important because if you get the directions wrong it puts a lot of strain on the nut.

There are many techniques for securing the strings to the tuning pegs. I prefer to run the string from the tailpiece through the hole in the tuning peg and pull it tight. Then I hold the string at the first or second fret to keep it tight at the tailpiece while I loop the string back around to where I ran it through the peg. Run it through, pull it tight and then tune up. This method won't leave a lot of slack string around the tuning post and has worked well for the last twenty years or so on my banjo.

Cut any extra string off the tuning peg with wire cutters or curl it by running the excess between your thumb and a nickel. Make sure that your fifth string wraps in the same direction as your fourth and third strings.

The Head

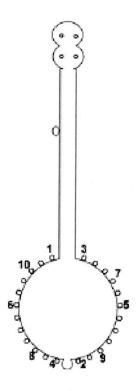

Another tricky part of banjo setup is tightening the head. The crazy thing about the banjo is that there is no standard for head size or head tensioning systems. Most modern banjos come with eleven-inch heads but this can vary from smaller than six inches to larger than thirteen inches in diameter. Banjo heads come in a wide variety of thickness and can be made of Mylar, calfskin and a bunch of other "stuff". It's up to you to decide what is right for your banjo but please don't start changing things until you have been playing for a while.

My rule of thumb regarding banjo head tension is that if you run your hand under the banjo head and can feel the feet of the bridge sinking into the head you might want to tighten it a little bit.

Your banjo head has to have an even tension all the way around. An easy way to make sure that you achieve this is to move back and forth across the head (see the diagram for an example) while you tighten the brackets. Just give a quarter of a turn each time. Take it slow and make sure that your head is even all the way around.

Don't get carried away. The only thing that sounds worse than a head that is too loose is one that is too tight.

To tighten your banjo head you will need either a bracket wrench (ask your local acoustic music shop) or a very small adjustable wrench.

Fingernail Care

In old time banjo we don't really need to use fingerpicks because nearly all of the playing is accomplished by striking the strings with your middle fingernail.

Most new banjo players go through some kind of fingernail angst because when you bang on a steel wire for any period of time your fingernail tends to break.

There are a lot of home remedies for thicker and stronger nails but I have never known any of them to work. Some players will go to a nail salon and have just their picking finger done. I have also heard some rather gross stories of banjo and guitar players trying to make artificial nails with pieces of ping-pong balls and crazy glue. That doesn't work and the crazy glue will really screw up your fingernail.

The best approach that I have found is to keep my picking nail at a reasonable length and just trim it a little bit or file it down if it gets torn or chipped. The less you think about your picking fingernail the less trouble you will have with it.

If you do break a nail and you need some volume for a jam session you can purchase a fingerpick at your local music shop and wear it over the top of your fingernail. Keep in mind that fingerpicks were not designed to be worn this way so you'll have to do a little bit of bending and twisting to make it fit.

General Supplies

You will need a strap for your banjo. Everybody has his or her own way of attaching a strap. I usually put the strap on the second bracket hook after the heel (next to #3 on the head tension diagram) and two brackets before the tailpiece (between #4 & #8 on the head tension diagram.) You want to put the strap over your head and with your right arm through the strap (or left arm if you are playing a left-handed banjo.) Tighten the strap so that it keeps the banjo neck up without any support from your fretting hand.

There are quite a few types of banjo straps available. I personally like to use a guitar strap. I just take off two bracket hooks, run the leather tabs of the guitar strap through the bracket hooks and put them back on my banjo. Some banjo straps have metal clips and others use leather tabs held in place by Chicago screws (how's that for a great name for a string band?) Shop around and use whatever feels good and fits your budget.

A music stand is another great tool to have. It will be a lot easier to follow the exercises in this book or play a tune from a songbook if you use a music stand. You can pick one up in any music store for a few bucks.

Sooner or later you will also need a capo. A capo is a clamp that fits on the fingerboard to make it easier to play in keys like **A** without retuning. Well, that's the idea. The truth is that most of the time you will have to check your tuning after you put on a capo because most models have a habit of putting your banjo out of tune.

There are many different types of capos on the market ranging from simple elastic band units that you can pick up for pocket change to ultra-fancy models costing several hundreds of dollars. The funny thing is that they all do the same job. I don't use a capo much anymore but when I *have* to I just use my guitar capo. I've found that a guitar capo works better because it is a lot bigger and as a result is less likely to put my banjo out of tune.

An instrument stand is a nice thing to have. While your banjo is a lot safer in its' case I have found that a banjo that is always in a case doesn't get played as much as a banjo kept within easy reach.

Another thing you need is a place to practice with an armless straight-backed chair. As you get more proficient with the banjo it won't matter what you sit on, how you sit or where you practice but in the very beginning you really want to have someplace to practice without any distractions so you can focus on what you are doing.

There are a lot of other setup issues. Things like a warped neck or a cracked heel (it happens) are best left to a good repair shop. Other issues may be unique to your banjo. Some banjos cannot be fixed. Use your head and don't get so focused on setting up your banjo that you never get around to playing. There is no substitute for practice. The most expensive banjo set up with the highest priced gadgets is useless if the person holding it cannot play.

For a complete overview of banjo setup you might want to check out the two and a half hour video <u>All About Your Banjo</u> by Karl & Sarah Dieterichs available at http://www.funkyseagull.com.

Basic Frailing

Now we are going to cover the basic frailing strum. This is the root of just about every down-picking banjo style. I know, right about now you want to know why it's called "frailing." I can't answer that question and neither could the folks who taught me. I never thought much about it because it's such a cool word. Anybody can "pick" a banjo but when you tell somebody that you are "frailing" it makes you sound like an expert even if you can't make it all the way through a song yet.

The basic frailing technique involves playing the first four strings of your banjo with the back of your middle fingernail while playing the fifth string with your thumb to create a quarter note and two eighth note rhythm. It's not a *hard* thing to do but it can feel a bit awkward in the beginning because we tend to think of playing the banjo as a matter of picking "up" with our fingers. It gets a lot easier with practice so just take this part of the book slow and easy.

First make sure your banjo is in tune. Then sit in a straight-backed chair with no arms. I know, the sofa or the recliner is much more comfortable but for now go along with me on this.

Sit up straight. I know that it is our natural inclination to slouch and some folks may say that it looks cooler but until you can do this in your sleep you need a dash of ritual and discipline in your practice time. So like I said, sit up straight.

Hold the banjo in your lap with the pot (or resonator) flat against your belly. Not off to the side, not on your knee. Use the banjo strap to support the banjo neck. You want your left (fretting) hand to be available when it is needed and that is going to be a lot sooner than you might think.

strike

Bring the banjo neck up so that the fifth peg is by your ear. If you were facing a clock you would want the neck at 10 or 11 o'clock.

For now your left hand isn't going to have much to do. Use it to cradle the banjo neck if you want (just remember that you really want to let your strap support the neck.) Chords come later and then your left hand is going to be very busy.

rear back

Hold your right arm out and make a fist. Now stick out your index finger and thumb just like when you were a kid playing cops and robbers. You want that sort of "gun" shape. Do not clench your remaining three fingers to your palm but rather try to relax and keep everything kind of loosey-goosey. Tension just slows things down.

The middle finger should be a hair extended.

Look at your hand. You've got your thumb up, your index finger straight out, your middle finger loosely curled and the last two fingers lightly touching your palm.

strike

Now that you've got your hand into a rough frailing shape drop that whole arrangement of fingers down onto the banjo head.

Put your thumb onto the banjo head so that you are just a little bit shy of touching the rim with the tip of your thumb. The pad of your thumb should be against the fifth string.

Rest your middle fingernail on the first string.

Now take a look at your hand and it's position on the banjo. You will see that you can just raise it up a hair and drop that middle fingernail down to strike the first string.

Do that a few times.

When you strike the first string do not flail around or open and close your hand or flick your fingers. Just use your thumb as a sort of pivot point to rear back (you won't have to go very far) and swing it down to strike the string with your nail. Let the string sort of snap off your middle fingernail.

Once you get comfortable with the idea of just dropping your hand down to strike the first string try the same thing on your second, third and fourth strings.

To hit those inside strings just look at your hand again. Your thumb is resting on the fifth string. If you close the webbing between your index finger and thumb you should see that you are able to position your hand so that it is over the string you want to hit.

We are not talking big motion here. It's just a hair this way and a hair that way. Don't be all stiff and rigid. Relax. Experiment with it for a while. You'll drive everybody in the house nuts but that's why you wanted to play the banjo, right?

After the strike comes the strum.

Strike any string. After you do that close the webbing between your thumb and index finger so that your hand comes back over the strings and your middle fingernail is over the third or fourth string. While all of this is happening keep your thumb in place.

Once you've reared back enough (three strings is a safe bet) strum down across the strings with your middle fingernail.

So it's pick, rear back and strum.

Do that a few times. Get used to it. Keep your thumb in place on the fifth string.

As you pick and as you strum it is a good idea to keep a sort of straight wrist. Your forearm is doing most of the work here using your thumb as a pivot point.

As you complete the strum you will see that your thumb is putting pressure on the fifth string. Snap your thumb off the fifth string with a rolling motion and drop it back in place.

Once your thumb drops back the pick and strum combination repeats. Remember to maintain hand position and to drive your hand across the strings with your forearm.

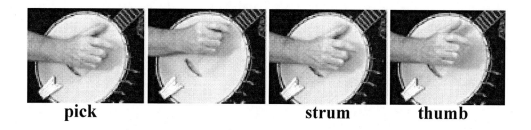

pick   **strum**   **thumb**

Do not flick your fingers. Play steady and slow.

A lot of little details of the stroke change from person to person. Our bodies all work in unique ways. I've got a buddy who adds a freaky little wrist flip after each down stroke. He can play very well so I figure there is no real point in asking him about it. It works for him and what I do works for me. *How* you do the strum isn't as important as playing in rhythm.

Let's give each major part of the frailing strum a label of some sort. We'll call the pick "**bump**," the strum "**dit**" and the thumb rolling off the fifth string "**ty**."

When you practice the basic strum it will help you get into the rhythm if you call out the name for each part of the strum.

On the strike say "**bump**."

Rear back for the strum, strum down and say "**dit**." As you are saying "**dit**" start rolling your thumb off of the fifth string and as the fifth string sounds say "**ty**."

Because the strum and the thumb happen right after each other we'll write it out as **bump dit-ty**.

Once you can play that picking pattern fairly well the next thing you want to do is get into the

bump   **dit**   **ty**

rhythm of the strum. We'll go over the actual note values in a little bit but for right now just try tapping your foot:

- On the **bump** tap your foot.
- As you tap your foot again do your **strum (dit.)**
- As your foot is coming back up thumb the fifth string for the **ty**.

So when you tap your foot it's **bump** (down & up) **dit** (down) and **ty** (up) (**tap tap-up.**) Play that a few times and try to keep everything even. It is going to take some time but you really need to be able to play this at a slow and steady rhythm. If you are constantly speeding up and slowing down it will make playing with other musicians all but impossible. Rhythm is everything. Without rhythm all we have is noise. Just kick back with your banjo for half an hour at a time and play the **bump dit-ty** rhythm over and over for a few days. Then you want to start working on playing a more varied picking pattern.

Play the first string on the **bump** until you can do it ten or twenty times in a row without interruption. Then strike the second string. Then try the third and fourth strings.

The **bump dit-ty** strum has a quarter note and two eighth note value. To get a better understanding of what that means we will take a look at note values.

Note Values

Do not panic when you see some sheet music in this section. We are not going cover *reading* music here. We are going to look at how note values are written in order to help you get a grip on the timing of the basic frailing strum.

In this chapter we are going to focus on 4/4 time. Things change a bit for 3/4 time and 6/8 time so we will cover those later.

The note value symbols are written in what is called standard music notation.

Music notation is written on a **staff**.

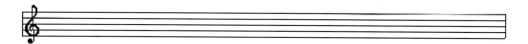

It is just five lines. Notes are written on the lines or in the spaces. The funky little squiggle at the beginning of the staff is a **G clef**. We will address what a **G clef** represents later on.

When you are writing music in standard notation each group of notes is broken up into a **measure**.

The **time signature** signifies the basic count for each measure.

In this case the 4/4 on the staff represents 4/4 time. That means four beats to a measure with the quarter note getting the beat.

A line running down through the staff marks measures. The example above shows four measures. In 4/4 time each measure is going to have four beats.

A *beat* is the term we use to describe the pulse of the music.

The really amazing thing about music is that those four beats can be broken up in all sorts of ways using whole notes, half notes, quarter notes, eighth notes and sixteenth notes.

A **whole note** is just that, a note that is counted for the whole value of the measure.

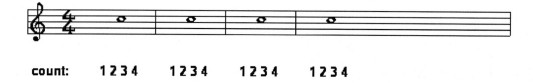

count: 1 2 3 4   1 2 3 4   1 2 3 4   1 2 3 4

A **half note** has one half the time value of a whole note.

count: 1 2   3 4   1 2   3 4   1 2   3 4   1 2   3 4

A **quarter note** has one half the time value of a half note.

count: 1 2 3 4   1 2 3 4   1 2 3 4   1 2 3 4

An **eighth note** has one half the time value of a quarter note.

count: 1& 2& 3& 4&   1& 2& 3& 4&

So when I say that the **bump dit-ty** strum has a value of one quarter note and two eighth notes it means the rhythm would look like this in standard notation:

bump   dit-ty   bump   dit-ty   bump   dit-ty   bump   dit-ty

1   2&   3   4&   1   2&   3   4&

Now if the **bump** has a quarter note value and the **dit** and **ty** have eighth note values that means the **dit** and the **ty** part of the strum both have to be half as long as the **bump**. This is because with an eighth note value the **dit** and **ty** together equal one quarter note.

Keep that in mind as you practice the basic strum.

And since this is the most important part of playing old time banjo let's go through the strum one more time:

- On the **bump** tap your foot. Bring your foot back up. ♩
- As you tap your foot again do your **strum**. ♪
- As your foot is coming back up thumb the fifth string for the **ty**. ♪

Your First Chord

If you have been practicing the basic frailing strum for a while I think it's safe to say that you and any people nearby are sick of hearing that open **G** chord. So let's give your left hand something to do by making chords.

Look at the back of your banjo neck. Imagine that there is a line running right down the middle of the neck from the headstock to where the neck meets the pot. When you grasp the neck to make a chord you want to put the joint of your thumb along that imaginary line. That will force your fingers to arch a little bit as they press the strings. This ensures that you won't start fretting two strings when you only want to fret one string (you will know what I'm talking about here in a few moments.)

Now with the joint of your thumb on that imaginary line fret (press) the **second string** at the **first fret** with your **index finger**. Keep your finger just behind the fret-wire. It might help if you realize that your finger is not doing anything but pushing the string onto the fret-wire. The fret-wire is higher than the fretboard so when you push the string down it stops vibrating right at the fret. That causes the string vibrations to shorten which results in a higher pitched note.

Strike the second string while fretting it at the first fret and listen. How does it sound? Is it a clear note like it was before you fretted the string? Is your first and third string sounding clear or is the finger on the second string muting them?

Adjust your hand a little bit so that when you fret the second string at the first fret your third and first strings are still clear and you are getting a clear note from the second string.

Once you have that sounding right keep your index finger on the second string first fret and use your **middle finger** to fret the **third string** at the **second fret.**

Strum the chord. Are all the notes clear? Once you get all of the strings sounding clear you have made a **D7 chord**.

On paper we'll use what's called a chord diagram to illustrate the chord forms. The box shows the first four strings of your banjo neck and the first four frets. The strings are numbered 4-3-2-1 (left to right) with 1 being your first string. The dark line on top represents the nut on your banjo neck. The two "0" symbols on top of the diagram tell you to play that string open. The black dots tell you where your fingers go.

You are going to have to work with this **D7** chord for a while. Our hands were not in any way, shape or form designed for this so you will have to train your fingers to do the job.

When you are making a chord keep in mind that you don't have to press too hard. A gentle touch will also help you in the speed department later. Light strings and a low action also help here.

Now hold that **D7** chord and play the basic **bump-dit-ty** strum. Once you are comfortable begin frailing the open **G** to **D7** back and forth. That is, a series of **bump-dit-ty's** in **G** and **D7** over and over again.

When you can do that we will play our first song.

Your First Song

We have covered a lot of ground so far.

- You can **tune** your banjo.
- You can play the **bump dit-ty** frailing strum
- You understand **note values.**
- You know the **G** and **D7** chords.

Let's start making some music.

Everybody knows the old song "**Skip To My Lou.**" It is a fun song to sing and play on the banjo. The really great thing about "**Skip To My Lou**" is that you only need to know two chords:

G
Lost my partner what'll I do?
D7
Lost my partner what'll I do?
G
Lost my partner what'll I do?
D7   **G**
Skip to my Lou my darling.

Now let's go back to our **bump dit-ty** (quarter note and two eighth notes) rhythm.

In 4/4 time that means two **bump dit-ty's** to a measure. So two measures would look like this:

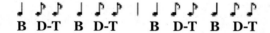
B D-T   B D-T   B D-T   B D-T

       B=bump D-T= dit-ty

Each line of "**Skip To My Lou**" is two measures long. So we know to play four **bump dit-ty's** in **G**, four in **D7** and so on.

What we are going to do here is sing and play the song. For now play any string for the bump. After you get more comfortable we'll go into playing the melody. Right now you want to get used to changing chords, playing the **bump dit-ty** strum and singing at the same time. Just **bump dit-ty**, **bump dit-ty** over and over again remembering to change chords at the right time.

Ready?   Let's go!

G

Lost my partner what'll I do?
B   D-T   B D-T   B D-T   B D-T

D7

Lost my partner what'll I do?
B D-T   B D-T   B D-T   B D-T

G

Lost my partner what'll I do?
B   D-T   B D-T   B D-T   B D-T

D7   **G**

Skip to my Lou my   darling
B   D-T   B D-T   B D-T   B D-T

Get that smooth and you can start adding more verses:

Skip, skip. Skip to my Lou. (3x*)
Skip to my Lou my darling.

I'll get another one prettier than you, etc.

Flies in the buttermilk shoo fly, shoo, etc.

Cat's in the cream jar what'll I do, etc.

*__*3x__ means sing it three times. I guess you could figure that out on your own,
but I once heard a guy sing "THREE X!" at a jam session.*

The C Chord

Let's go over what you should know by now.

- You can **tune** your banjo
- You know the basic **frailing strum**
- You know your **note values**
- You know two **chords**
- You can sing and play the chords to "**Skip To My Lou**."

My advice right now is to reach around and give yourself a nice big pat on the back. To any bozo on the street you **are** a banjo player. There is a lot more to learn but you have made great progress.

All right, that's enough basking. Back to work.

Make your **D7** chord.

If you remember my explanation of how to make a **D7** chord your index finger is fretting the second string at the first fret and your middle finger is fretting the third string at the second fret.

What we are going to make now is a *partial* **C** chord. It is a partial chord because we won't be fretting or using the fourth string. In fact, you will see an "x" over the fourth string in the chord diagram. We'll go over the "full" **C** chord later on.

If you look at the **C** chord diagram and the **D7** chord diagram you will see that all you have to do to switch from **D7** to **C** is move your middle finger from the **third** string second fret to the **first** string second fret. You can go back and forth from **D7** to **C** without ever letting go of the second string at the first fret.

Is that cool or what?

What I want you to do now is work on changing from **G** to **D7** to **C** while playing the **bump dit-ty** strum. Then work on other combinations like **C** to **D7** to **C** or **G** to **C** to **G** to **D7** until you are comfortable with various combinations.

Now that you are able to combine the **C** chord with the **G** and **D7** chords we can get started on another song.

Just about everybody has heard the old song "**Red River Valley**."

While "**Skip To My Lou**" was a two-chord song "**Red River Valley**" ups the ante to three chords. We will approach this song pretty much the way we covered "**Skip To My Lou**." I will mark out the measures, chord changes and the rhythm over the lyrics for you. You can play whatever string you want for the **bump** in your **bump dit-ty**. We won't be playing the melody yet. Just remember that a quarter note and two eighth notes equal a **bump dit-ty**.

There are a couple of pick up notes at the beginning of this song. When you start singing "From this valley they say . . ." do not start playing your **bump dit-ty** until the word "**valley**." Note that the last **bump dit-ty** of the song is actually the pick-up notes for the next verse.

"Red River Valley"
4/4 Time Key of G

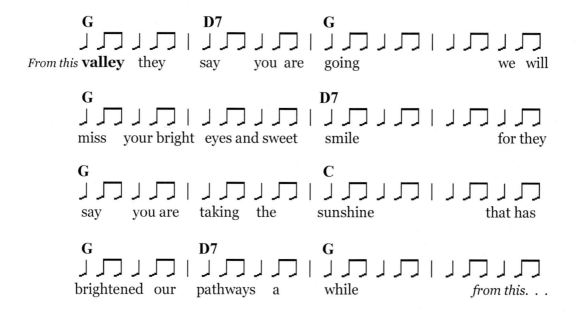

Come and sit by my side, if you love me,
Do not hasten to bid me adieu,
Just remember the Red River Valley,
And the cowboy who loved you so true.

I've been thinking a long time, my darling,
Of the sweet words you never would say,
Now, alas, must my fond hopes all vanish?
For they say you are going away.

Do you think of the valley you're leaving?
Oh how lonely and dreary it will be.
Do you think of the kind hearts you're breaking?
And the pain you are causing to me?

They will bury me where you have wandered,
Near the hills where the daffodils grow,
When you're gone from the red river valley,
For I can't live without you I know.

Get used to the rhythm of this tune. Then experiment with your **bump dit-ty's**. See if you can find the melody notes on your own. They are all there, right in or near the chord forms. Also try it with "**Skip To My Lou**." Spend some time with these songs. Get to know them. Get comfortable with the rhythm and the chords. **And don't forget to sing!**

The F Chord

Let's go over what you know so far:

- You can **tune** your banjo
- You know the basic **frailing strum**
- You know your **note values**
- You know three **chords**
- You can sing and play **"Skip To My Lou"** *and* **"Red River Valley!"**

You're doing great so let's keep going.

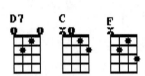

I have added the partial **F** chord to our **C** (partial) and **D7** diagrams. Take a look at all three. The **F** chord is just a **D7** with your ring finger fretting the first string at the third fret.

Get used to switching from **C** to **F** to **G** and back to **F** along with your **bump dit-ty** strum.

When you are able to do this smoothly without interruption we can tackle a new song.

"Boil Them Cabbage Down" is a funky little song in **C**. The lyrics are a hoot and it's a great exercise to get you playing in the key of **C**.

If you go back and look at **"Skip To My Lou"** and **"Red River Valley"** you will notice that I am giving you a little bit less of a walkthrough for each tune.

This time I have marked out the measures in the song lyrics (look for the '|' symbol) and given you the chord progression. By now you should have gotten the idea that in 4/4 time each measure has two **bump dit-ty's**.

The only thing you want to watch out for with this song is the next to last measure. It has one **bump dit-ty** for the **C** chord and one for the **G** chord.

Play the entire song on the **first string** and you will be playing the melody. The only exception is that the very last **C chord** is played on the **second string**.

Let 'er rip and remember to **sing**!

"Boil Them Cabbage Down"
4/4 Time Key of C

C   F   C   G

Went up on a | mountain | to give my horn a | blow

C   F   C G   C

Thought I heard my | true love say | yonder comes my | beau!

Chorus:

Boil them cabbage down, down
Bake some hoecakes brown, brown
The only song that I can sing
Is boil them cabbage down

Someone stole my old coon dog
I wish they'd bring him back
He'd chase the big hogs through the fence
And the little ones through a crack

Possum in a 'simmon tree
Raccoon on the ground
Possum said "you son of a gun
Throw some 'simmons down!"

Once I had an old gray mule
His name was Simon Slick
He'd roll his eyes and back his ears
And how that mule could kick

I have no idea how many other verses are out there but this is one of those songs that you can sing and play all night long.

Once you get used to playing this in the key of **C** why not work it up in the key of **G**?

"Boil Them Cabbage Down" in the key of **G**:

Sorry, but the first string trick won't work for the melody here. Just strum anywhere as you sing. Then have some fun and try to find your melody notes.

"Boil Them Cabbage Down"
4/4 Time Key of G

G   **C**   **G**   **D7**
Went up on a | mountain | to give my horn a | blow

G   **C**   **G**   **D7**   **G**
Thought I heard my | true love say | yonder comes my | beau!

Play this one a couple of hundred times and when you're ready we can start picking a little bit of melody.

Melody & Rhythm

Let's go over what you know so far:

- You can **tune** your banjo
- You know the basic **frailing strum**
- You know your **note values**
- You know four **chords**
- You can sing and play **three songs**,
  one of them in *two* different keys!

We've come a long way. By now you should be comfortable playing the frailing strum while singing and changing chords. The next step is to add a little bit of melody.

In order to illustrate the examples in this chapter I will have to introduce you to something called tablature. Tablature, or 'tab' for short, is just a way of writing a song down.

You have five lines. Each line represents a string on your banjo. The fifth string is at the bottom and the first string is on top.

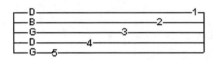

When any string has a zero you play that string open. The numbers on a string tells you what fret to play. So in this example you would play your fifth string at the fifth fret, your fourth string at the fourth fret, your third string at the third fret and so on. A series of numbers running one on top of the other tells you to strum a chord (**dit.**)

In order to make things easier I will add a rhythm line over some of the tab files in this chapter. A measure of **bump dit-ty's** in open **G** looks like this.

And this shows the same measure in **C**.

Note: The strum (**dit**) portion of the frailing stroke will *usually* be made out of a chord form.

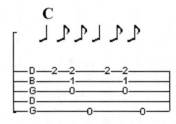

Pretty cool isn't it?

So if we go back to "**Boil Them Cabbage Down**" in the key of **C** and put it into tab we wind up with this:

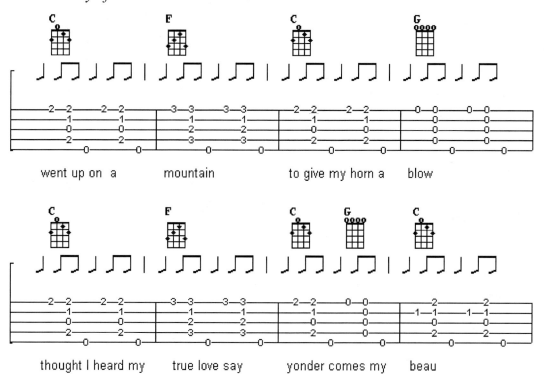

went up on a   mountain   to give my horn a   blow

thought I heard my   true love say   yonder comes my   beau

With the exception of the last measure everything here is pretty much like it was *without* the tab. You will notice that the chord diagrams show the *full* **C** and **F** chords as opposed to the partial chords you are using now. I'm going to keep showing the full chord diagrams from this point on but I will leave it for you to decide when to start using them. The partial chords will work 99% of the time and it's a heck of a lot easier in the beginning.

One thing to remember if you keep using partial chords is that when a song is written out in tab it is just a suggestion. If you see a note that you cannot play comfortably in a tab change it. As long as the rhythm remains constant it will work just fine and dandy.

As we continue playing melody let's take a look at **hammer-on's** and **pull-off's**.

As I've been saying over and over again, your basic frailing **bump dit-ty** strum contains a quarter note and two eighth notes.

This can sound kind of monotonous after a while. So to add a little bit of spice to your banjo stew we can take that quarter note and break it in half. One way to do that is to use the **hammer-on**. Rather than go into a long explanation here let's just play a couple.

Strike the open first string and play a **bump dit-ty**. When you strike that first string drop your middle finger onto the first string at the second fret. The trick here is not to change the rhythm.

In tab it would look like this:

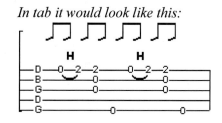

Now if you look at the rhythm line you will notice that the quarter note for the bump has become two eighth notes. That's why a **hammer-on** is so cool. It is coming in and slicing the quarter note into two even pieces

♩♪♪   becomes   ♪♪♪♪

A **pull-off** works under the same idea but in a **pull-off** you are playing a *fretted* string and then snapping your finger away from that string.

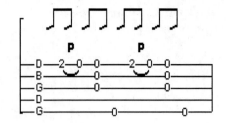

Both of these techniques change the sound from **bump-dit-ty** to **bump-a-dit-ty** but the basic rhythm stays the same.

Let's take a look at what something as simple as a **hammer-on** can do for a song.

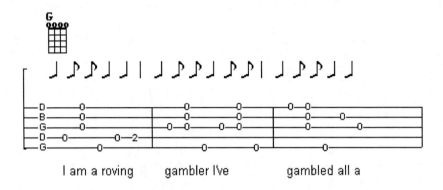

I am a roving   gambler I've   gambled all a

In this clip from "**Roving Gambler**" the melody is pretty straightforward. The first measure has a **bump dit-ty** followed by two quarter notes.

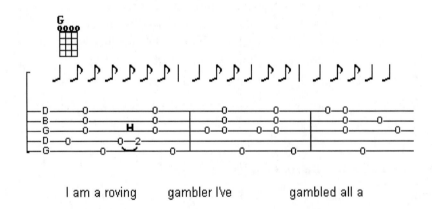

I am a roving   gambler I've   gambled all a

In this second clip I changed the two quarter note run into a **hammer-on**. Because the **hammer-on** is two eighth notes I had to add a **dit-ty** strum to even out the measure.

That's the trick. No matter what you do to dress up the measure it still has to come out even. A measure in 4/4 time **must** have a value equal to four quarter notes.

Since we're talking about the song "**Roving Gambler**" we might as well play it.

"Roving Gambler"
4/4 Time Key of G

G
I am a roving | gambler I've | gambled all | around
                                    C   **G**
when I see | a deck of cards I | lay my money | down.

As with the songs earlier in the book I have broken **Roving Gambler** into measures and marked out the chord progression. This is a pretty simple song to **bump dit-ty** along with because in the first six measures you are just playing your open **G** chord then one measure of **C** and one last measure of **G**.

Once you can sing the verse and play a simple rhythm you can start to experiment with blending the melody into the basic strum. I have tabbed out a simple arrangement that you can use for ideas. Just remember that this is a *suggestion*. It is up to you to experiment and make the song sound the way that *you* want it to sound.

"Roving Gambler"
4/4 Time Key of G

I am a roving   gambler I've   gambled   all around

when I see   a deck of cards I   lay my money   down

> **I've gambled down in Washington I've gambled over in Spain**
> **I'm on my way to Georgia to knock down my last game.**

> **When I was down in Washington many more weeks than three**
> **I fell in love with a pretty little girl and she fell in love with me.**

The neat thing about frailing a song like "**Roving Gambler**" is that the melody line sort of floats right along with the rhythm. That is the real magic of old time banjo. It is just as strong playing solo as in a group setting.

But that is not the only thing happening with "**Roving Gambler**."

If you look at the tab again you will see that even with only a single **pull-off** you are still getting much of the melody just by changing the string that you use to start the **bump dit-ty**.

With that idea in mind go back and take another run through "**Skip To My Lou**" and "**Red River Valley**." See if you can get a feel for the melody by changing the string that you use to start the **bump dit-ty**.

Another kind of hammer-on is something I like to call the "**phantom**" hammer-on. A **phantom hammer-on** works when you **strike** one string but **hammer-on** another string.

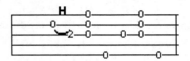

Another technique that is related to the **pull-off** and the **hammer-on** is the **slide**.

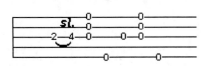

A **slide** is when you strike a string and while it's still ringing drag your finger down one, two or more frets. The trick to a slide is not to release the pressure on the string. Try it and you will see what I mean.

Just like the **pull-off** and the **hammer-on** a slide is another way to split a quarter note into two eighth notes.

Now go back and look at "**Boil Them Cabbage Down**" again. When we played that song we did it as simply as possible by just running the **bump dit-ty** over and over again. So what would happen if we added a **hammer-on** or **pull-off** to emphasize the phrasing of "**Boil Them Cabbage Down**?"

We can already play the tune *straight*:

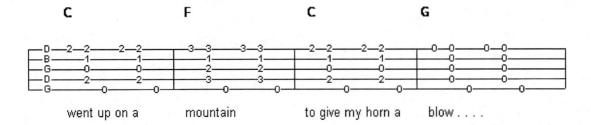

That works just fine but what if you decided to use a **hammer-on** at the second string, first fret?

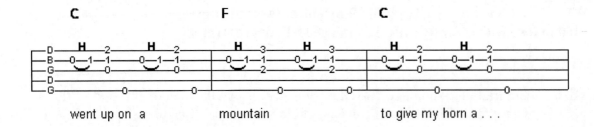

Now why not try a **pull-off** on the first string?

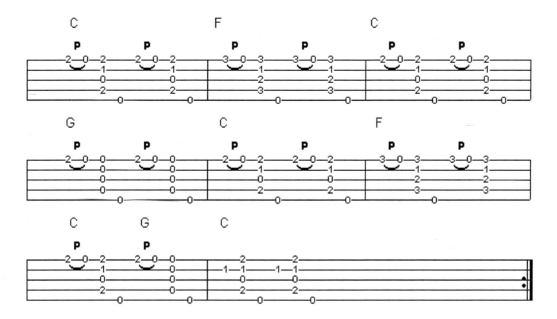

Now, if that works on the first string and the fourth string is tuned to the same note as the first string (**D**) then you could try something like this:

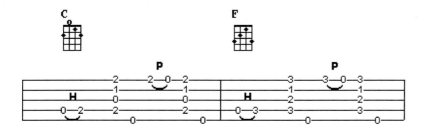

What can you do with the third string? Would a **slide** from the third string, second fret to the fourth fret sound good? Keep these thoughts in mind as we start to learn some more songs.

Putting It All Together

Let's go over what you know at this point.

- You can **tune** your banjo
- You know the basic **frailing strum**
- You know your **note values**
- You know four **chords**
- You can sing and play **four** songs one of them in *two* different keys!
- You can read **tab**
- You can play **hammer-on's**, **pull-offs** and **slides**.

Now we are going look at some simple tunes to see how everything covered up to now blends together.

"Handsome Molly"
4/4 Time Key of C

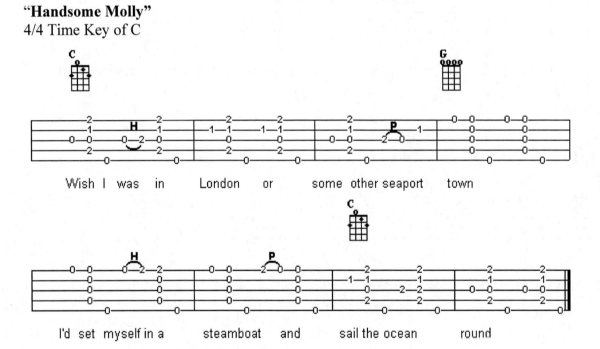

Wish I was in London or some other seaport town

I'd set myself in a steamboat and sail the ocean round

> While sailing on the ocean, while sailing on the sea
> I'd think of Handsome Molly wherever she might be.

> She rode to church on Sunday, she passed me on by
> I could tell her mind was changing by the roving of her eye.

> Don't you remember Molly, when you gave me your right hand?
> You said that if you should marry that I would be the man.

> Now you've broke your promise go love whom you please
> While my poor heart is breaking you're lying at your ease.

Some performers use the second line of each verse as a chorus when they sing "**Handsome Molly.**" For example, the last verse would have a chorus like: "*Lying at your ease, lying at your ease. While my poor heart is breaking you're lying at your ease.*" You will have to decide for yourself whether or not to use the chorus. There is really no right or wrong way to do it.

When you sit down to work on "**Handsome Molly**" my advice would be to just play a simple rhythm the first few times through. Once you are comfortable with the chord progression start adding the melody line from the tablature.

I cannot emphasize enough how important it is to sing while you are playing these songs. In order to do that you are going to have to sit up straight while you are playing. You cannot sing while all hunched over looking at your hands.

As a matter of fact you don't want to look at your picking hand at all. Trust me, looking at your picking hand is not going to make you any more accurate. Accuracy isn't the issue here. You *are* going to make mistakes. Getting all tensed up about it will just set you up to make *bigger* mistakes on a more regular basis.

You will get some benefit from looking at your fretting (left) hand. The visual input will enhance the development of the "muscle memory" needed to change chords quickly.

When you work on "**Handsome Molly**" and the other tunes in this book try to relax. If you make a mistake just keep going.

When you sing don't be all tentative and soft or squeaky. **Sing!** Don't be embarrassed or shy. And don't sing through your nose. Sing from your belly with your diaphragm pushing the air through your voice box.

Keep things at a nice even tempo. Playing fast is a lot of fun but it is easy to loose control. What sounds "just right" to you may sound rushed and muddled to your audience.

The next two songs are "**Old Rattler**" and "**Mountain Dew**" in the key of **C** and in **G**. Both of these songs are somewhat similar to "**Handsome Molly.**" The melody line is there but it is the rhythm that makes the song work.

"Old Rattler"
4/4 Time Key of C

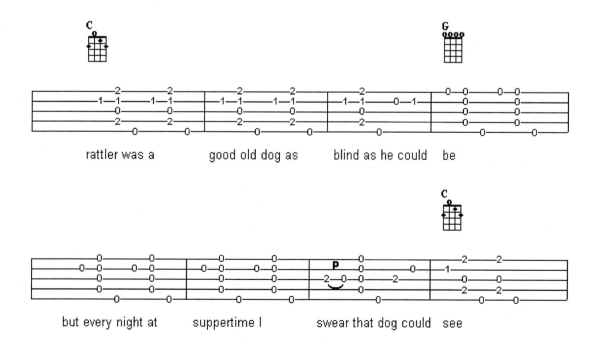

Here Rattler here, here Rattler here.
Call old Rattler from the barn here, Rattler here.

Rattler barked the other night I thought he'd treed a coon.
When I come out to find him he's barkin' at the moon.

Mountain Dew"
4/4 Time Key of G

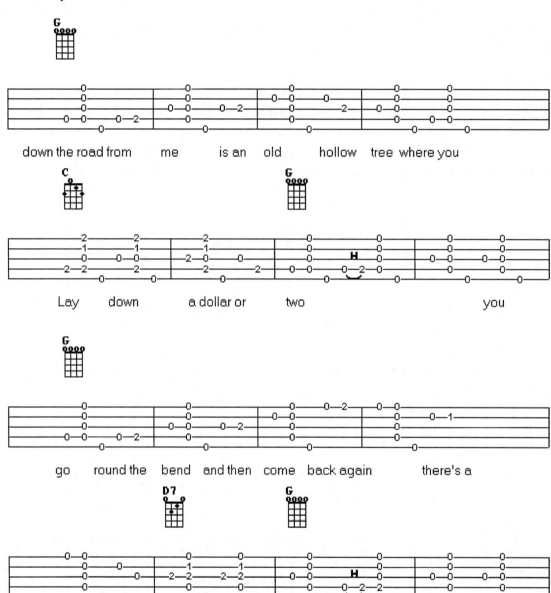

down the road from   me   is an   old   hollow   tree   where you

Lay   down   a dollar or   two   you

go   round the   bend   and then   come   back again   there's a

jug   of that   good   old mountain   dew!

Chorus:
They call it that good old mountain dew, yes they do!
And them that refuse it are few.
I'll hush up my mug if you fill up my jug
With that good old mountain dew.

Well my uncle Bill has a still on the hill
Where he runs off a gallon or two.
Buzzards in the sky get so drunk they can't fly
From sniffin' that good old mountain dew!

My cousin Nort he is sawed off and short
He stands about four foot two.
But he thinks he's a giant if you give him a pint
Of that good old mountain dew!

Old preacher Brown he did rode into town
Said his wife had a touch of the flu.
He thought that I ought just to sell him a quart
Of that good old mountain dew!

Our next song is "**Sugar Hill**." It is a pretty easy tune but it has a new chord form for you learn.

Think of the **E minor** chord as a **C** chord with the second string open.

Minor chords have a sort of sad sound about them and in some settings they can sound almost menacing. It all depends on how you use the chord. In a song like "**Sugar Hill**" things lean a bit more to the menacing side.

"Sugar Hill"
4/4 Time Key of G

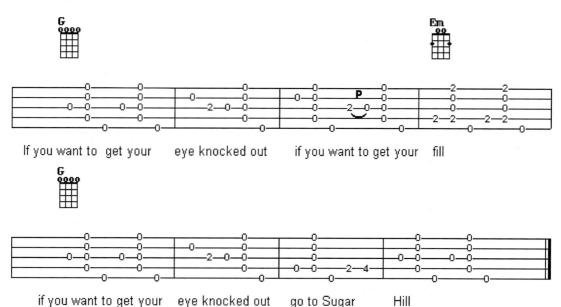

If you want to get your   eye knocked out   if you want to get your   fill

if you want to get your   eye knocked out   go to Sugar   Hill

**I'm getting lonesome for my gal. I want a drink of rye.
I'm a-going to Sugar Hill or know the reason why.**

**Get your banjo off the wall. Grab your fiddle, Bill.
Hitch the horses to the sleigh, we're going to Sugar Hill.**

The next song is "**Going Down That Road Feeling Bad**" This is a genuine classic. Musicians as diverse as Blind Lemon Jefferson, Bruce Springsteen and Woody Guthrie have written their own lyrics for this one. It is one of those songs that everybody seems to know. Best of all it's as easy to play as falling off a log.

I'm going down that   road   feeling   bad   yes I'm

going down the   road   felling   bad   yes I'm

going down the   road   feeling   bad   lord   lord   and I

aint   gonna   be   treated   this   a   way

I'm going where the water tastes like wine.
I'm going where the water tastes like wine
I'm going where the water tastes like wine Lord Lord
And I ain't gonna be treated this a way.

I'm going where the weather suits my clothes, etc.

They fed me on cornbread and beans, etc.

By the time you have worked through these five songs you should be able to see that there is a pretty similar picking pattern through each of them. You really are not doing anything all that different from just playing the basic strum as we did for "**Skip To My Lou**" and "**Red River Valley**".

Believe it or not, almost everything in old time banjo falls into this pattern. You will change it a little bit here and there. Maybe once in a while instead of playing the **bump dit-ty** strum you will use a **slide**, **hammer-on** or a **pull-off** to change the rhythm to **bump-a dit-ty.** Maybe you will play four quarter notes instead of two **bump dit-ty** strums in order to fill out a measure. Maybe you will leave out part of the strum and just leave an empty spot with the note value of what you would normally play. In the long run no matter what you do it's just a variation of the basic strum.

Pretty wild isn't it?

Let's go through some more songs. The root of all of these tunes will still be the **bump dit-ty** strum but we will start adding more single note runs, slides and other variations. If you have trouble with a measure just do your basic strum and try it again later.

"**Cripple Creek**" is one of the songs you almost *have* to be able to play. It is an old fiddle tune that has become sort of the unofficial anthem for banjo players everywhere. This tune also introduces the basic format that most fiddle tunes follow.

You will see that the verse and the chorus have been labeled A and B. The traditional way to play a song like this is A twice and then B twice. This is not a hard and fast rule. Some fiddle players will break it up as AAB or ABAB. It just depends on how the group you are playing with decides to do it.

"Cripple Creek"
4/4 Time Key of G

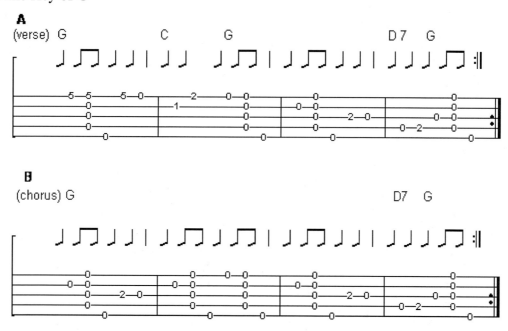

*The :|| *symbol is a repeat sign.*

I've got a gal at the head of the creek
Going up to see her at the end of the week

Chorus
Going up Cripple Creek going in a run
Going up Cripple Creek to have some fun

Girls on Cripple Creek 'bout half grown
Jump on a boy like a dog on a bone

"**Little Maggie**" is a popular old tune that you will run into at bluegrass jams. This is a good one to practice your slide on. The chord progression is kind of unusual.

"Little Maggie"
4/4 Time Key of G

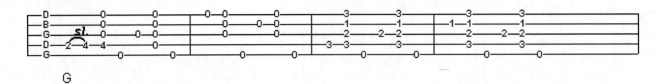

Over yonder stands little Maggie
With a dram glass in her hand.
She's drinking away her troubles
She's courting another man.

The first time I seen little Maggie
She was sitting by the banks of the sea.
Had a forty-five strapped 'round her shoulder
And a banjo on her knee.

Now she's marching to the station
With a suitcase in her hand.
She's going for to leave me
She is bound for some distant land.

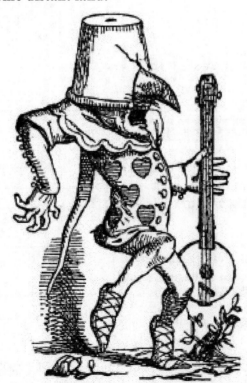

36

"**Wildwood Flower**" is a song that you rarely hear anybody sing anymore. The lyrics are a bit cryptic but it has managed to become a favorite country guitar instrumental piece.

"Wildwood Flower"
4/4 Time Key of G

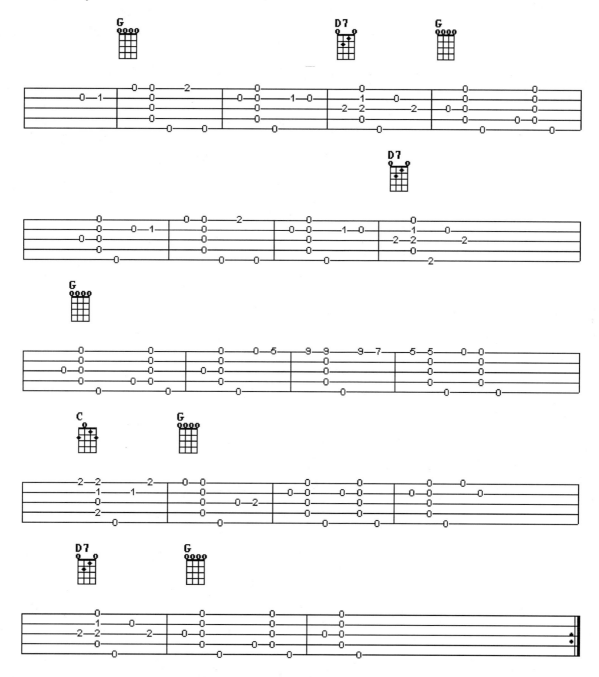

I will twine and will mingle my raven black hair
With the roses so red and the lily so fair
And the myrtle so green with it's emerald hue
The pale emanita and the eyes look so blue.

Like I said, the lyrics are kind of cryptic. I have seen folk singers argue for forty-eight hours straight about the meaning of the lyrics to "**Wildwood Flower**."

Before you head on to the next chapter spend a good bit of time with these tunes. You want to be able to keep an even rhythm through the entire song. Singing along while you play will go a long way toward making that happen.

Try not to worry about making a mistake and if you *do* make a mistake keep going. In a band or a performance situation you cannot stop the music and say, "Oops, let me do that again!"

Music is a lot like a river. You have to keep rolling with it. If you pause to think about a note you will spend the rest of the song trying to catch up. Everyone you are playing with will think you are some kind of a dipstick because nothing on earth is quite as hard to listen to as a band with someone playing out of time.

So don't worry about playing the song perfectly. If your rhythm is correct and you are following the chord progression you <u>cannot</u> make a mistake. For the next few weeks you should work on being able to sing and play these songs all the way through without breaking the rhythm. If you hit a wrong string keep going. If you flub a chord keep going. If you forget a part of the song just play your **bump dit-ty** and follow the chord progression until you remember where to go next.

Taking A "Break"

By now you have been playing the tunes from the last chapter for a while so it's time to start making everything a little bit more polished.

Up to this point you have been working on songs that involve either playing simple rhythm or perhaps an arrangement that has a bit of a melody line. Either will work fine but as you gain better control of your banjo you will want to add some dynamics to your playing.

By dynamics I mean not just playing the same thing over and over again. It is hard to sing and play melody at the same time and it is boring to play straight rhythm without your voice carrying the melody. The answer is to have two versions of the same song. A back up version to use when you are singing and a melody line version for when you want to take a solo or a "break."

One thing to keep in mind is that your banjo does not have to be quite as loud when you are singing as when you are taking a lead break. By that I mean you can begin to lighten up your right hand attack when you are singing. You want to use the banjo to *support* your voice rather than overpower it.

Now let's create a back up and a lead version for "**The Wreck of the Old 97.**" This classic bluegrass and old-time country tune is also a true story. We met a gentleman from Virginia several years ago who lived between Lynchburg and Danville. He remembered the day that Old 97 went off the track!
The way I usually play this one is to sing a verse / play an instrumental / sing a verse over and over again until the song is finished.

In the tab for the break you will run into a new chord.

A **D** chord is nothing more than your **C** chord moved down two frets. It looks different at first because your third string is open when you make a **C** chord but look at it again. I'll explain how this works later.

"The Wreck of the Old 97" <u>**Back-up**</u>
4/4 Time Key of G

they gave him his orders in Monroe Virginia saying

Steve you're way behind time this is

not thirty-eight but it's old ninety - seven you've got to

put her into Danville on time

Wreck Of The Old 97
Instrumental Break

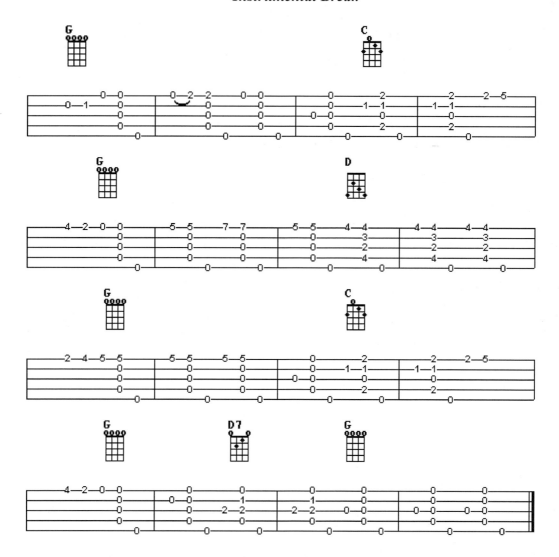

Well he turned and he said to his black & greasy fireman
"Just shovel on a little more coal,"
and when we cross that White Oak Mountain
you can watch Old 97 roll!"

Break

It's a mighty rough road between Lynchburg and Danville
On a line with a three-mile grade
It was on this grade that he lost his air breaks
You can see what a jump that he made.

Break

He was coming down that grade making ninety miles an hour
When his whistle turned into a scream.
He was found in the wreck with his hand on the throttle
He was scaled to death by the steam.

Break

The telegram came from the Lynchburg station
And this is what is said,
"That daring engineer who ran Old 97
Is lying near Danville dead"

Break

So ladies you must heed my warning
And from this day now on learn
You must never speak harsh words to your true loving husband
He may leave you and never return.

There is another kind of break that is used once in a while in old-time banjo, something I like to call the "joke break" or the "story break."

A classic example of this is "**Arkansas Traveler**." The tune itself is easy enough but what makes this one so much fun is that it is an old comedy routine probably going back to medicine show days.

This song takes two people to make it work so you will have to talk a friend into doing the routine with you. The idea is that one person (the banjo player) is a farmer picking a banjo on his porch by the side of the road. The other character is a traveling salesman who has managed to get lost. As the routine opens up the banjo player runs through this little tune:

"**Arkansas Traveler A Part**"
4/4 Time Key of G

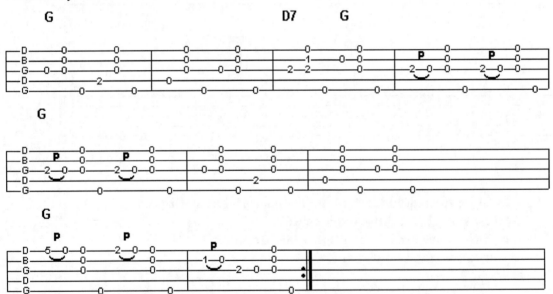

After you play the **A** part of the song once through the salesman kicks in with his part of the routine:
Salesman: "Hello there. Say, which road do you take to Nashville?"
Farmer: "I think they've got a road in Nashville already."

Play Tune

Salesman: "I mean can I take this road to Nashville?"
Farmer: "I'd like to see you try. It's awful heavy."

Play Tune

S: "So have you lived here all your life?"
F: "Not yet."

Play Tune

S: "Say, your roof looks like it needs mending.
   Why don't you fix your roof?"
F: "Can't fix it when it's raining, and when it's not raining it don't leak."

Play Tune

S: "You're not very smart are you?"
F: "Well, I'm not lost."

Play Tune

S: "I mean there's not much between you and a fool is there?"
F: "Just this banjo."

Play Tune

S: "Your corn is growing tall in the field.
   Do you put manure on your corn?"
F: "No. We use butter like everybody else."

Play Tune

*If you are doing this routine with another banjo player
you can end it like this:*

S: "Say there, why do you keep playing that first half of the tune
   over and over again?

F: "First half? I've been looking for years hoping that   somebody would
   show me the rest of this song!"

S: "Well let me see that banjo." *Plays the **B** part of the tune*:

Arkansas Traveler <u>B Part</u>"
4/4 Time Key of G

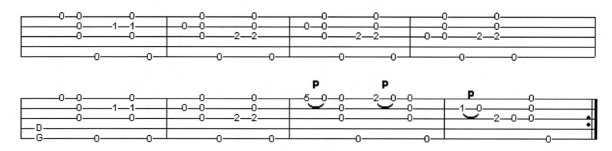

Farmer: "Wow! Have you been playing all of your life?"
Salesman: "Not yet . . ."

There are quite a few songs and routines like this. Grandpa Jones and Uncle Dave Macon performed a lot of them at The Grand Old Opry. You can always make one up one of your own. On the old TV show Hee-Haw they used to tell awful jokes between quick versions of "**Cripple Creek**."

You could rip through "**Cripple Creek**" and after one time though say:

Did I ever tell you about my cousin Johnny-Boy?   Well, when he was a little kid he would not talk.   In fact up until he was eight years old he had never said a word!   Then one day he was at the dinner table and he looks up and says; "Hey, These potatoes are cold!"

Well his momma jumped up waving her arms in the air and said, "Praise the Lord!   Johnny-Boy, you can talk after all!   Now how come you haven't said a word in the past eight years?" Johnny-Boy just shrugged his shoulders and said, "Everything's been all right up 'till now."

And then tear through "**Cripple Creek**" again

You might as well start working on entertaining people because once your friends find out that you can play the banjo they will drive you half crazy to play something for them.   Like an old burlesque comedian told me years ago "The audience doesn't care how good you *play*, just how good you make them *feel*."

Chord Forms

Bar Chords

By now you should be comfortable with some basic chords:

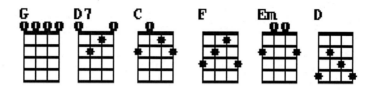

As you may have noticed you can make a lot of music with this handful of chords but there is plenty more cool stuff on the fretboard. The easiest way to explore all of the chords available on your banjo is to use **movable chords**.

The easiest **movable chord** to use is the **bar chord**. Since your banjo is tuned to an open **G** chord all you have to do is lay one finger across the fretboard to make a new chord:

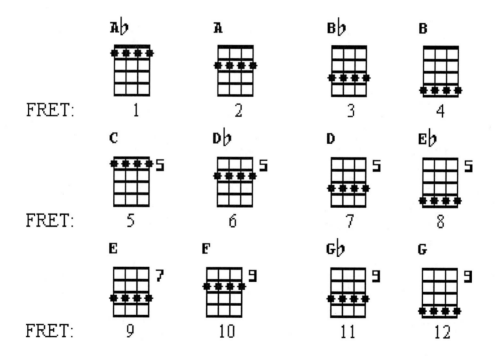

  And if both of these chords are G7, it's easy to figure out how to make a seventh chord from any of the other bar chords.

You can also use this chord chart as a capo placement guide. By placing the capo at the second fret any song played as you would in the key of **G** is changed into the key of **A**. If we go by this chart what key would we wind up playing in if the capo was on the fourth fret?

If you said "**B**" you got it right.

Just keep in mind that the fifth string will have to be tuned up in order to match the new key. If you capo at the second fret you must tune the fifth string to **A**. This will match the first string at the fifth fret **but now your fifth fret is actually the seventh fret.**

Once you start using a capo beyond the fifth fret there is really no need to retune the fifth string because the capo will hit all five strings. Your first string and your fifth string will wind up matching but if you try it you will find that it works reasonably well.

Before we move on to the other movable chord forms let's play a couple of songs that use bar chords.

"**Lynchburg Town**" was the first tune I ever figured out using a bar chord.

"Lynchburg Town"
4/4 Time Key of C

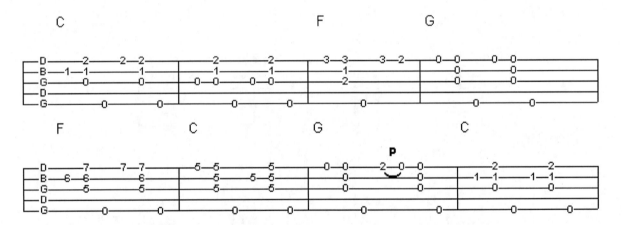

       Going down to town, going down to town.
       Going down to Lynchburg town
       To lay my tobacco down

"**The White House Blues**" is fun to play but a lot of people, myself included, have had a heck of time with this one. The jump from the barred **C** chord to **F** is tricky but if you walk the chord in (make a D7 first *then* fret the first string) it's not too bad.

"The White House Blues"

4/4 time, key of C

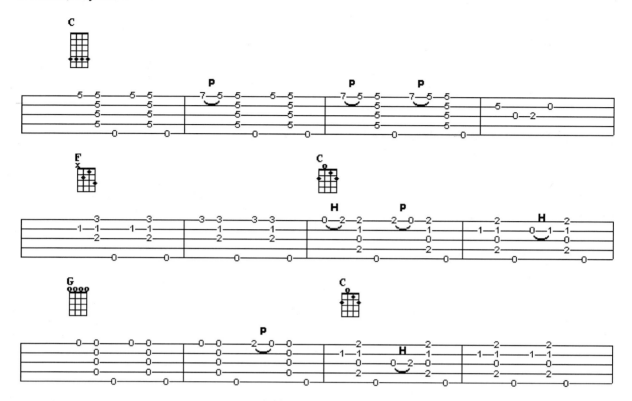

McKinley hollered McKinley squalled.
Doc said, "McKinley I can't find that ball.
You're bound to die in Buffalo."

Doc came a running pulling off his specs.
Doc said McKinley "You better cash in your checks
you're bound to die in Buffalo."

Look here you rascal see what you done.
You shot my husband with your Iver Johnson gun.
I'm takin' you back to Washington.

Hush now you children don't you fret.
You'll draw a pension at your daddy's death.
From Buffalo to Washington.

Forty four boxcars trimmed in lace.
Put him the last one so we can't see his face.
From Buffalo to Washington.

Before we continue I think I should point out a really neat thing about this song. **"The White House Blues"** is about the assassination of President McKinley at the Pan American exposition. The melody for the song was taken from another topical song about the McKinley administration called **"The Battleship Maine"** that dealt with our brief war with Spain after the Maine was destroyed either by accident or on purpose. **"The Battleship Maine"** is a great song in it's own right and is a lot of fun to play before or after its younger brother **"The White House Blues."** It is also an interesting example of the folk process at work.

47

"The Battleship Maine"

McKinley called for volunteers so I got my gun.
First Spaniard I saw coming I dropped my gun and run.
It was all about that Battleship Maine.

Why are you running are you afraid to die?
The reason that I'm running is because I cannot fly.
It was all about that Battleship Maine.

The peas they were greasy the meat it was all fat.
The boys were fighting Spaniards while I was fighting that.
It was all about that Battleship Maine.

The next song we are going look at is an old fiddle tune called "**Ragtime Annie**." In the first three measures all you have to do is hold your **C** chord and **hammer-on** the third string at the second fret. The rest of the song is pretty self-explanatory. I usually play this one **AABB** just like we did with "**Cripple Creek**." There are no words to this tune that I know of.

"Ragtime Annie"
4/4 Time Key of G

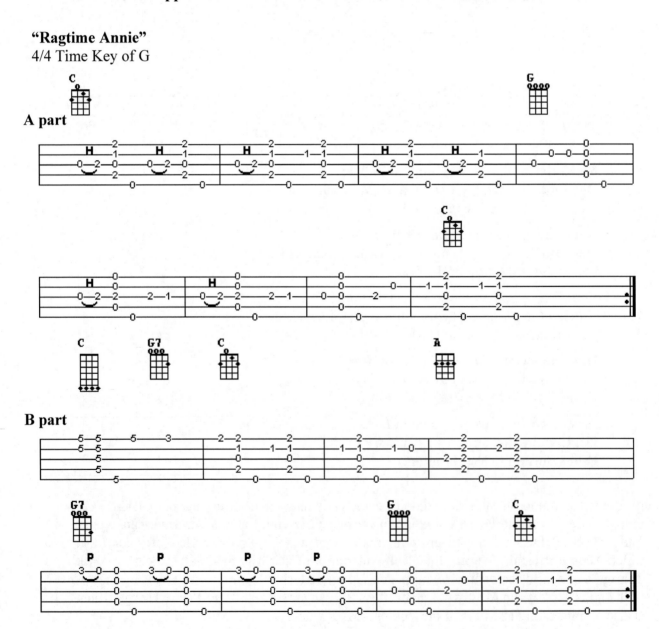

Another exercise to help you get used to working with bar chords is to practice moving a lick up and down the fretboard.

This little lick is really a piece of the **G** scale. I usually play the notes in the first two measures as quarter notes and use a whole note in the third measure. The lick is easy to remember if you think of it as a takeoff of your **D7** chord.

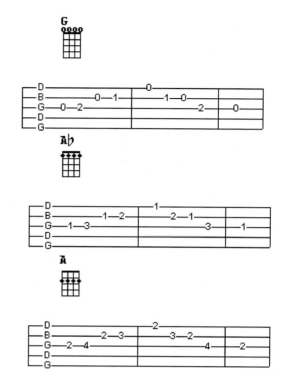

Now we are going to make a bar chord across the first fret (an **A♭** chord) and play the same lick that we used in the first example.

Move up the neck one fret to an **A** chord at the second fret.

Try doing this over and over again all the way to the twelfth fret (where you will wind up playing the lick in **G** again) and then work your way back towards the nut.

Make up some licks of your own with this exercise.

Before you move on to the next chapter try the songs we have covered up to this point with a capo. You might also want to try experimenting with playing a few simple tunes like "**Boil Them Cabbage Down**" just using your **bar chords**. You can start out with open **G** and use the **C** chord at the fifth fret and the **D** chord at the seventh fret as in this example:

"Boil Them Cabbage Down"
4/4 Time Key of G

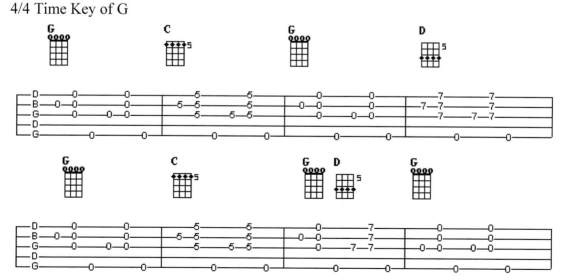

Or use the **G** chord at the twelfth fret:

"Boil Them Cabbage Down" *4/4 Time Key of G*

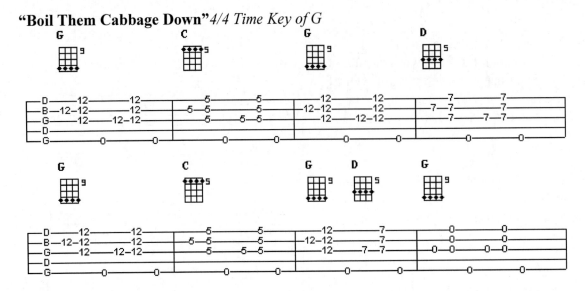

To play this song in **C** using bar chords just start with the **C** chord on the fifth fret and slide down to the **F** chord at the tenth fret. I will give you the first couple of measures to get started. You can finish working out an arrangement on your own:

"Boil Them Cabbage Down"
4/4 Time Key of C

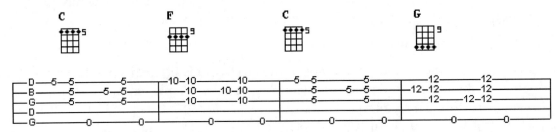

If you want to try something *really* different you can stop by your local guitar shop and pick up a **slide** or a **bottleneck**. **Slides** and **bottlenecks** come in a wide variety of shapes and sizes but they all work under the principal of using a piece of metal or glass on your finger to do the fretting.

If you do try a guitar slide keep in mind that you do not push the slide down on the fretboard. Just let the slide lightly touch the strings directly over the fret.

It's a lot of fun and you can get some crazy sounds. Try it!

You don't even have to buy a slide. You can get pretty much the same effect with a pocketknife or a cigarette lighter. The late, great electric guitar player Danny Gatton was known to play slide solos with a pizza crust that he would snatch from a table in the audience!

Use your imagination but be at least a little cautious not to damage your banjo. I don't want to get any calls from repair shops complaining about trying to get pepperoni grease out of a fretboard.

The C, F & Minor Chord Positions

C

D

The **C position** is another movable chord form.
We've been using the **C** chord quite a bit throughout this book and in the last chapter I introduced you to the **D** chord.

The interesting thing about a **D** chord is that it is just the **C** chord moved up the neck two frets. The reason it looks different at first glace is that in your **C** chord the third string is open but it is fretted at the second fret in the **D** chord. The reason that happens is simply because you ran out of fretboard at the nut.

Let's move that **C** chord around a little and see what we get:

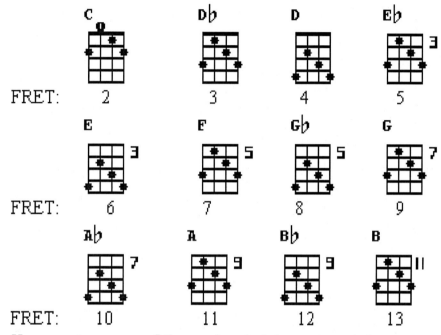

C	Db	D	Eb
FRET: 2, 3, 4, 5

E	F	Gb	G
FRET: 6, 7, 8, 9

Ab	A	Bb	B
FRET: 10, 11, 12, 13

You can turn any of these chords into a seventh by changing one note:

C7

FRET: 3

This works anywhere on the fretboard.

Your capo can come into play here as well. As we said before if you capo at the second fret anything that you play in **G** winds up in **A**. Well that also means anything you play in **C** winds up in **D**. Try it.

Now, if you use a capo at the fourth fret and play in **C** what key would you wind up in?

If you said the key of **E** give yourself a cigar.

One really odd thing about the **F** position is that the first chord in the **F** position is actually an **E** chord.

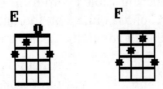

This is, hopefully, a clue as to how a capo works with a chord position. We started exporting that idea in the last chapter and if you peek ahead and look at **"Flop Eared Mule"** you might get some more ideas about how you can mix your basic chord forms with the **G**, **C** and **F** position chords when you start playing up the neck.

Here is your **F** position chord chart:

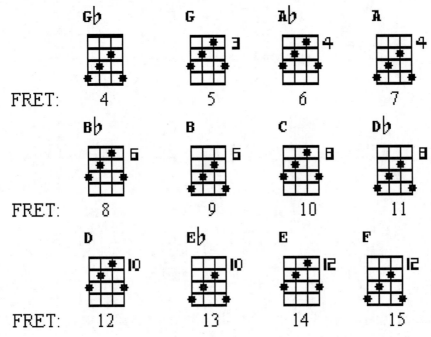

Once again, any of these chords can be made into a seventh by changing one note:

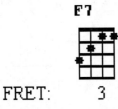

In order to get comfortable playing in the **C** and **F** positions anywhere on the fretboard you can try playing combinations of **C** and **F** position chords up and down the neck.

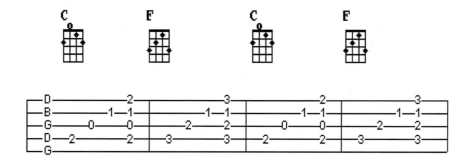

```
 D--------------2--------  --------3--------  --------2--------  --------3--------
 B----------1--1--------  --------1--1------  --------1--1------  --------1--1------
 G------0--------0------  ----2--------2----  ----0--------0----  ----2--------2----
 D--2------------2------  --3----------3----  --2----------2----  --3----------3----
 G----------------------  ------------------  ------------------  ------------------
```

In this example we are just using the **C** and **F** chords that you already know. We are not playing a **bump dit-ty** here. We are picking three single notes and a strum with each part of the measure having a quarter note value (4/4 time.)

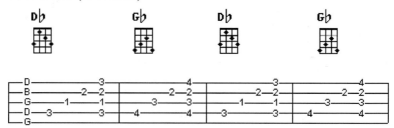

```
 D--------------3--------  --------4--------  --------3--------  --------4--------
 B----------2--2--------  --------2--2------  --------2--2------  --------2--2------
 G------1--------1------  ----3--------3----  ----1--------1----  ----3--------3----
 D--3------------3------  --4----------4----  --3----------3----  --4----------4----
 G----------------------  ------------------  ------------------  ------------------
```

In this example we have moved both chord positions up the neck one fret. Our **C** chord becomes a **Db** and our **F** chord becomes a **Gb**.

Keep moving this exercise up the neck to the twelfth fret and then work your way back towards the nut.

Minor chords also have several movable forms.

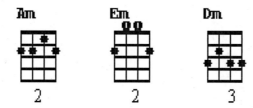

FRET: 2   2   3

Just like the major chords each of these position are moveable.

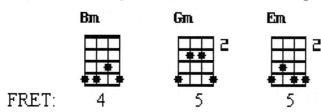

FRET: 4   5   5

You can use the previous chord charts to find where these minor chord forms can be used.

Before you move on to the next chapter you may want to experiment with mixing up your **G**, **C**, **F** and **minor** position chords.

Soon we will be talking about playing within a "**box**" on the fretboard. A little advance work here will pay off later.

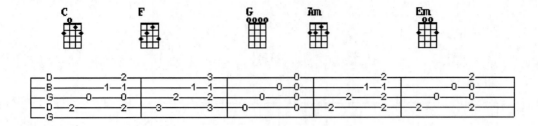

In this example we are using the same picking pattern as in earlier examples but we are adding three other chord positions into the mix.

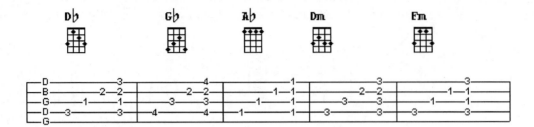

Just like the earlier exercise we are moving everything up the neck one fret each time through. Try this one up to the twelfth and drag it back towards the nut.

54

Playing In 3/4 Time

Everything up to this point has been played in 4/4 time. Now we are going to take a look at the other major time signature used in old time banjo.

3/4 is also referred to as waltz time.

As you already know, 4/4 time is four beats to the measure with the quarter note getting the beat.

3/4 time is *three* beats to the measure with the quarter note getting the beat.

What this means is that the **bump dit-ty** (1 2&) becomes **bump ditty-ditty** (1 2& 3&)

```
D—0—0———0————————0————0—
B———0———0————0—0——0—
G———0———0————————0————0—
D——————————————————————————
G——————0————0————0————0—
```

The hardest part of frailing in 3/4 time is getting the feel of the strum. You have spent so much time getting the **bump dit-ty** down cold that changing it into **bump ditty-ditty** (a quarter note and four eighth notes) can feel a little awkward at first. Stick with it and take it slow. You will be waltzing along in no time.

 We'll go through "**Who's Gonna Shoe Your Pretty Little Foot**" nice and easy. Play it just like your other basic tunes. Hit any string and play the basic strum
(in this case **bump ditty-ditty**.)

"Who's Gonna Shoe Your Pretty Little Foot"
3/4 Time Key of G

G

Who's gonna	shoe your	pretty little	foot?
bump ditty-ditty	bump ditty-ditty	bump dtty-ditty	bump ditty-ditty
1 2& 3&	1 2& 3&	1 2& 3&	1 2& 3&

C   **G**

Who's gonna	glove your	hand?	
bump ditty-ditty	bump ditty-ditty	bump ditty-ditty	bump ditty-ditty
1 2& 3&	1 2& 3&	1 2& 3&	1 2& 3&

C   **G**

Who's gonna	kiss your	red ruby	lips?
bump ditty-ditty	bump ditty-ditty	bump ditty-ditty	bump ditty-ditty
1 2& 3&	1 2& 3&	1 2& 3&	1 2& 3&

D7   **G**

Who's gonna	be your	man?	
bump ditty-ditty	bump ditty-ditty	bump ditty-ditty	bump ditty-ditty
1 2& 3&	1 2& 3&	1 2& 3&	1 2& 3&

Poppa will shoe my pretty little foot
Momma will glove my hand.
Sister will kiss my red ruby lips
I don't need no man.

I don't need no man poor boy
I don't need no man.
Poppa will shoe my pretty little foot
I don't need no man

The longest train I ever did see
Was sixteen coaches long.
The only girl I ever did love
Was on that train and gone.

Once you get past the awkward feeling of the new picking pattern 3/4 time shouldn't give you too much trouble.

Lets run through a few more tunes while looking at how the melody notes fit into the strum.

Now that you are comfortable playing **bump ditty-ditty** in 3/4 time try this arrangement of **"Who's Gonna Shoe Your Pretty Little Foot."**

"Who's Gonna Shoe Your Pretty Little Foot"
3/4 Time Key of G

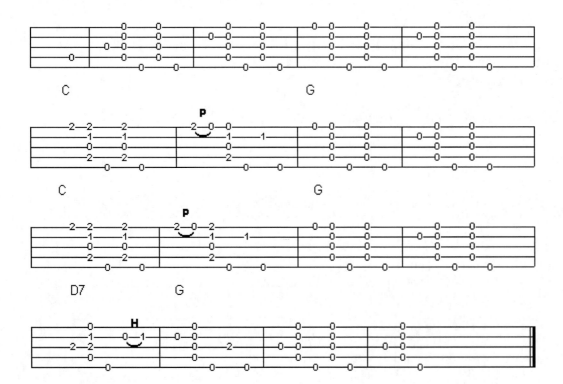

As you can see there is not a whole lot going one here but the melody is still coming out clearly over the rhythm.

Just as in 4/4 time the real trick here is simplicity. The melody line never gets so complicated that you have difficulty keeping the rhythm smooth and steady.

Take a look at the next song "**In The Pines**." The structure of this tune is very close to "**Who's Gonna Shoe Your Pretty Little Foot**" You are playing a 3/4 time **G**, **C** and **D7** chord progression in both songs but they sound very different from one another.

"In the Pines"
3/4 Time Key of G

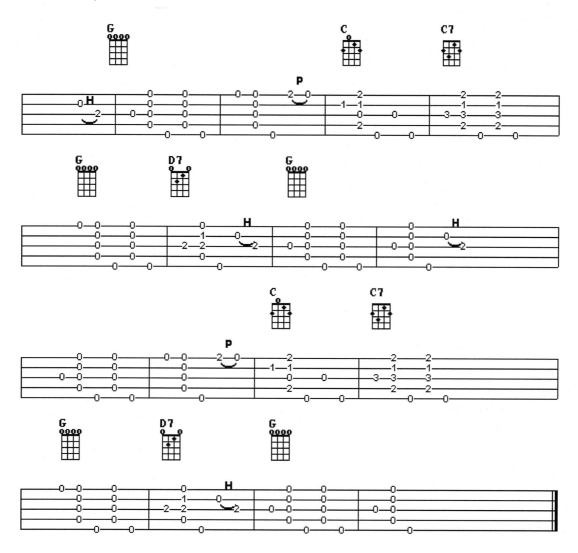

Little girl, little girl don't lie to me
Where did you sleep last night?

In the pines, in the pines
Where the sun never shines
And I shivered the whole night through.

"Farther Along"
3/4 Time Key of G

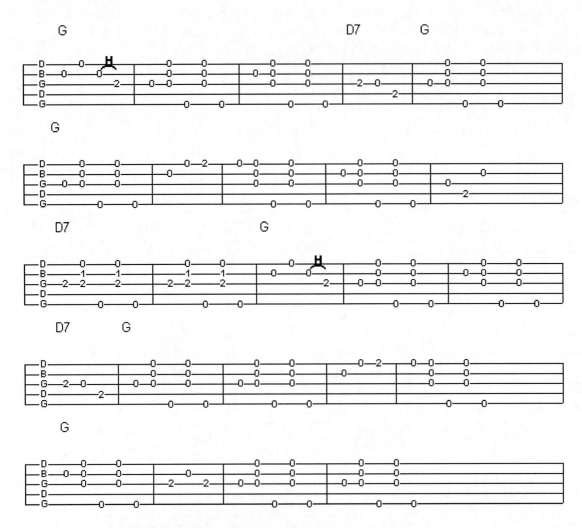

Tempted and tried, we're oft made to wonder
Why should it be thus all the day long
While there are others living about us
Never molested, though in the wrong

Chorus:
Farther along we'll know all about it.
Farther along we'll understand why.
Cheer up my brothers live in the sunshine.
We'll understand it all by and by.

"Rosin The Beau"
3/4 Time Key of G

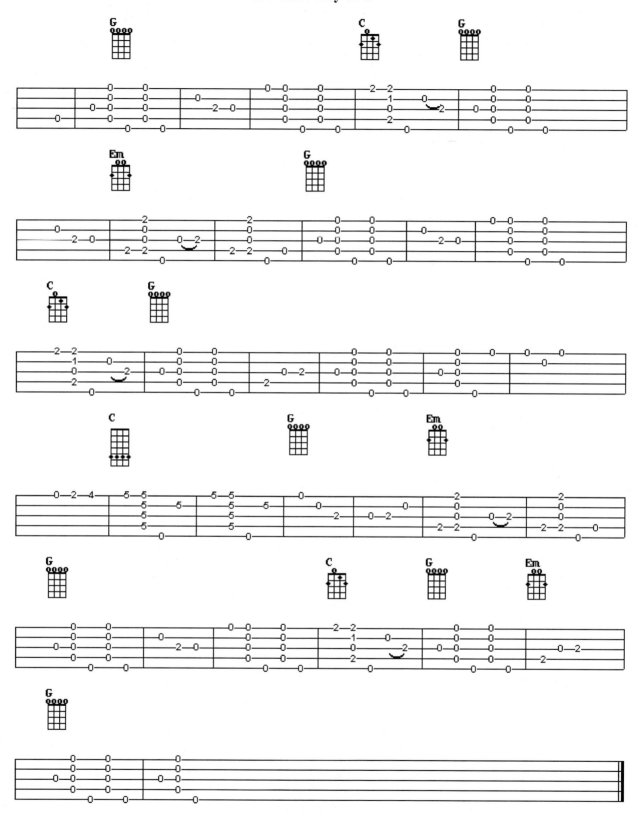

"**Rosin The Beau**" is another one of those tunes with more than one set of lyrics. The song was most likely played as an Irish air a long time ago. The first set of lyrics might not have been written until the late 1700's or the early 1800's.

"Rosin The Beau"

I've traveled this world all over
And now to another I go,
And I know that good quarters are waiting
For to welcome old Rosin the Beau.
To welcome old Rosin the Beau
To welcome old Rosin the Beau
I know that good quarters are waiting
For to welcome old Rosin the Beau.

When I'm dead and laid out on the counter,
A voice you will hear from below,
Saying send down a hogshead of whisky
To drink with old Rosin the Beau.
To drink with old Rosin the Beau
To drink with old Rosin the Beau
Saying send down a hogshead of whisky
To drink with old Rosin the Beau.

When Abraham Lincoln was running for president somebody wrote new words and used the melody to come up with a campaign song.

"Lincoln And Liberty"

Hurrah for the choice of the nation
Our chieftain so brave and so true
We'll go for the great reformation
For Lincoln and Liberty too!
We'll go for the son of Kentucky
The hero of Hoosierdom, too!
The pride of the "Suckers" so lucky
For Lincoln and Liberty too!

There are a few other songs that use the melody from "**Rosin The Beau**." I hardly ever sing any of them because to me, this is probably the prettiest banjo instrumental I have ever run across.

Drop Thumb & Double Thumb

Double Thumb

Another little piece of right hand trickery is a technique called the **double thumb**.

Just like a **hammer-on** or a **pull-off** the **double thumb** is used to cut the time value of a note in half but the application is different. You see, sometimes you are going to run into a lick that needs a little bit of spicing up and a **hammer-on** or a **pull-off** just won't *feel* right.

For instance, this single note run is made up of **quarter notes**. It sounds fine and it will work in most situations, but it doesn't *feel* fast.

By thumbing the fifth string after each single note the quarter notes are cut in half so you wind up playing a string of **eighth notes**. The time value stays the same but it *feels* a lot faster.

The timing for this can be tricky at first. Give yourself some time to practice.

Used with some taste this is probably one of the most powerful techniques in the old time banjo players' bag of tricks.

Double thumbing can turn the simplest lick or run into a showstopper. Not because this is hard or super complex but because it fools the listeners ear into thinking that there a lot of *stuff* going on. You may just be playing a note and following it up with the fifth string but it sounds so fast that everything sort of blurs together and your audience will think that you are doing something really complicated.

A good way to build up your understanding of when to use **double thumbing** might be to look at how a flatpicking guitarist plays a solo. Part of the speed in flatpicking comes from the ability to pick up and down very fast on a string. In frailing we are only working with a down stroke. Doubling each single note with the fifth string creates the illusion of that flatpicking effect.

You can use the **double thumb** anywhere that you have a single note or a run of single notes. **Double thumbing** can also be used to add an accent note.

Here are a couple of licks that you can use to practice your **double thumb** technique.

This first lick is one I used to play over and over again when I was working on my **double thumb** technique. I would walk up and down my driveway for hours running this lick. I just about drove my neighbors crazy.

Working the **double thumb** on the fourth string can feel a little bit awkward at first because you are dealing with such a small space. Get this lick clean at a super slow pace and then start speeding it up.

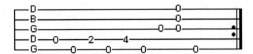

This lick will help you get used to walking the **double thumb** across the strings.

Drop Thumb

Another interesting right hand technique is the **drop thumb**.

Just like the **hammer-on**, **pull-off**, **slide** and **double thumb,** *drop thumb* is used to break up the **bump dit-ty**.

Drop thumb is different because while the other techniques change one part of the basic strum, <u>drop thumb</u> <u>changes the entire picking pattern.</u>

In the **basic strum** you are picking with your middle fingernail, strumming down with your middle fingernail and plucking the fifth string with your thumb.

In **drop thumb** you are striking a string with your middle fingernail, striking a string with your thumb, striking a string with your fingernail and then thumbing the fifth string.

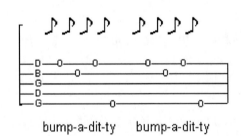

bump-a-dit-ty   bump-a-dit-ty

By changing the picking pattern you change the rhythm of the strum into a string of eighth notes. The thumb rolling down to play a melody string gives the motion an entirely different *feel* and that is the problem with **drop thumb**. In order for it to really work well you need to have your rhythm playing skills rock solid. There is nothing quite as awesome as **drop thumb** played well but there is nothing quite as pathetic as **drop thumb** played badly. If you want to use this technique you are going to have to put in a *lot* of practice time.

Start working with your open **G** chord. Then go on to changing chords while keeping the rhythm smooth.

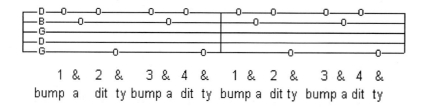

```
 D—0———0———————0———0———————0———0———————0———0—————
 B———————0———0———————0———————————0———0———————0———
 G————————————————————————————————————————————————
 D————————————————————————————————————————————————
 G—————————0———————0———————————0———————0——————————
```

```
   1 &  2 &   3 & 4 &    1 &  2 &   3 & 4 &
 bump  a  dit ty bump a dit ty bump a dit ty bump a dit ty
```

Try playing "**Boil Them Cabbage Down**" using the **drop thumb**.

You don't have to play the **drop thumb** exactly as it is written here. Any combination of strings will work as long as your rhythm stays consistent.

"Boil Them Cabbage Down"
4/4 Time Key of C

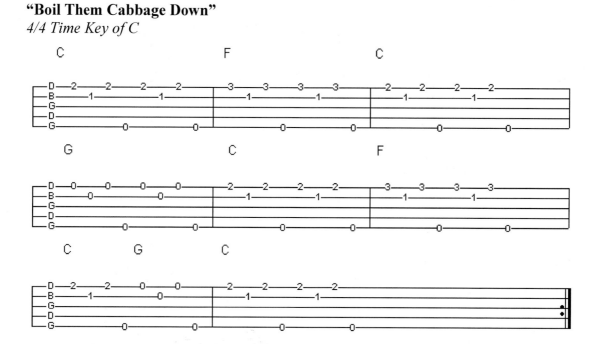

```
     C                        F                    C
 D—2———2———2———2———3———3———3———3———2———2———2———2—
 B———1———————1———————1———————1———————1———————1———
 G————————————————————————————————————————————————
 D————————————————————————————————————————————————
 G—————————0———————0———————————0———————0———————————0———————0—
```

```
     G                        C                    F
 D—0———0———0———0———2———2———2———2———3———3———3———3—
 B———0———————0———————1———————1———————1———————1———
 G————————————————————————————————————————————————
 D————————————————————————————————————————————————
 G—————————0———————0———————————0———————0———————————0———————0—
```

```
     C        G          C
 D—2———2———0———0———2———2———2———2—
 B———1———————0———————1———————1———
 G————————————————————————————————
 D————————————————————————————————
 G—————————0———————0———————————0———————0—
```

Try playing "**Flop Eared Mule**." If the **drop thumb** parts give you trouble just put in a **bump dit-ty** instead.

"Flop Eared Mule"
4/4 Time Key of G

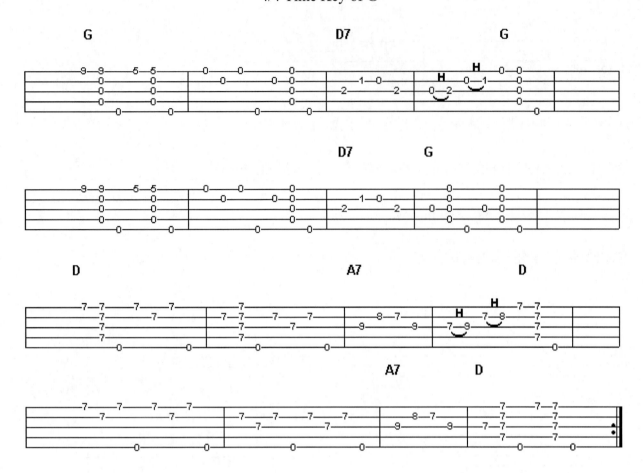

Bends & Vibrato

Bending a string is a simple enough concept. You just fret a string and while it's ringing keep pressure on the string with your fretting hand and give it either a push or a pull across the fretboard.

What this does is change the pitch of the sting but you don't get an exact note. You get sort of an "in between" note.

Try it. Fret your third string at the second fret. Now play that third string and while it's still ringing keep fretting the string but give it a nice easy push over towards the fourth string.

Now try it the other way around. **Bend** the string before you play it and while it is still ringing ease it back to its normal position.

It's going to take you some time to develop a touch when it comes to **bending** strings. There really isn't any way to tab out an exercise on paper that would make sense. Your best practice tool is to just mess around with the idea. With a little bit of practice this can be a powerful technique. You can even substitute a **bend** for a **slide** in some songs.

Vibrato is similar to **bending** in that both techniques involve pushing a fretted string around. However, instead of changing a strings pitch **vibrato** is all about sustain. Sustain means how long a note will "hang" in the air. The five-string banjo was never designed to have a lot of sustain. You hit a note and it's gone. But in some songs you are going to want at least a little bit of sustain. That's where **vibrato** comes in.

In order to add a touch of **vibrato** all you have to do is wiggle your finger around while you are fretting a string. Sometimes when I am using this technique I might just move my finger back and forth like a fast **bend**. Other times I might let go of my banjo neck entirely except for the string that I am fretting and let my whole hand rock back and forth. The weight of my hand swinging moves the string around on the fret just enough to give the impression that the note is sort of hanging in the air.

Chopping & Vamping

Chopping and **vamping** are techniques that you can use in your rhythm playing.

Chopping is a variation of strumming. In 4/4 time you might simply play four quarter note strums counting 1-2-3-4

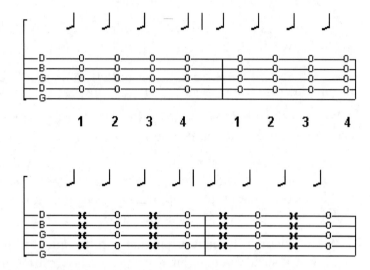

When you **chop** the idea is not to play anything for the 1 and the 3 count of the measure. So you would play:
rest-strum-rest strum or
1- **chop** 2- **chop**.
Notice that this is not the **bump dit-ty** strum. We are just brushing down the strings with the middle fingernail here. I usually leave my thumb on the fifth string for this but you can try it in different ways and use what works best for you.

You are still playing a 4/4 time rhythm but it feels a little bit different. Chopping creates a sort of tension behind the music. This is one reason that bluegrass mandolin players use the technique so much.

You may notice that the chop sounds kind of goofy with an open chord on your banjo because the strings keep ringing. A way to enhance the chop is to play "full" chords (chords that use all four strings) along with a left hand technique called **vamping**.

To **vamp** a chord let your fingers lighten up and return to the strings right after the strum. This cuts the ringing of the chord short. Try using an **F** position **G** chord (look at the chord chart earlier in the book) to practice your **chopping** and **vamping** with "**Little Maggie**" and "**Cripple Creek**"

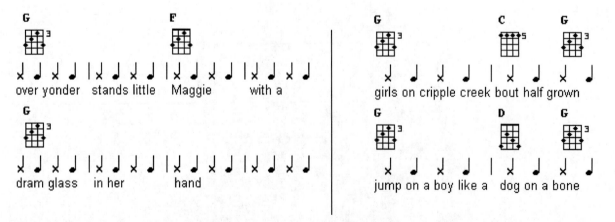

Try this technique on any of the other tunes in this book. It is a great trick to use in a jam session. I've also found it useful to throw a measure or two of chopping and vamping into songs that I play and sing solo.

Other Rhythm & Volume Tricks

As soon as you tried your first **hammer-on** and **pull-off** you changed the basic strum into something different. That should be a clue that once you have internalized the basic rhythm of frailing banjo there is plenty of room to change things around even more.

The **chop** is one example of this. When we chopped we treated the rhythm as four quarter notes but we only played every other beat. When we covered **double thumbing** and **drop thumbing** we took the strum out of the **bump dit-ty** and changed the rhythm to **bump-a-dit-ty**. This changed the rhythm of the measure from two **bump dit-ty** strums to a string eight eighth notes.

There are other ways to change the basic frailing strum. In what is often today referred to as clawhammer banjo the **bump dit-ty** rhythm stays the same but the strum is often left out and a pause (or rest) with a time value of an eighth note is substituted.

A **rest** is a pause in the music with a time value. A **rest** can have the time value of any note. It is easy enough to do. You just don't play anything.

━ **whole note rest** ━ **half note rest** ₹ **quarter note rest** ❼ **eighth note rest**

In this simplified example we have a typical **bump dit-ty** with an **eighth note rest** replacing the **dit** (strum.)

Where and how you use **rests** depends on the song and what effects you are trying to achieve.

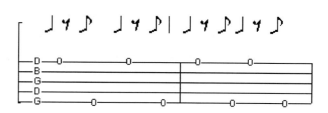

There are other ways to change or enhance the rhythm of a song. You could let your picking hand strike or brush the banjo head at the end of the **bump dit-ty** or **chop**. You could let the heel of your hand mute the strings right after the strum **(dit)** portion of the **bump dit-ty**. I have even seen guys stop playing altogether and use both hands to bang on the banjo head like a bongo drum.

You can change the feel of parts of a song without altering the rhythm by rising or lowering the volume of your banjo. It's simple enough to hit with a harder or softer touch when you are playing the **bump dit-ty** but it doesn't end there. You can change the tone even more by altering the location of your right hand. If you play close to the bridge you will get a somewhat sharper sound. As you move closer to the neck you will find the tone getting softer. Some folks will play all the way up over the fretboard.

Volume is a real issue on the banjo because by it's nature it is a pretty loud instrument. That is not a bad thing exactly. In fact I think that it is the raw power of the instrument that draws people to it. However, when you are singing or playing back up you don't want the banjo to be fighting the music so you may want to start working on controlling the instrument.

Go back through the earlier chapters and run through some of the tunes again but this time work on the idea of toning down the volume when you are singing and bringing it up when you are playing a break. This will take some time to master but the long-term results are really worth the effort.

Licks

A lick is a little snatch of a tune. It is a banjo "sound effect" that can be used in a variety of ways. You can string a few different licks together to create an arrangement or use just one lick in your rhythm playing to emphasize your singing.

Licks also have another important role in learning to play the banjo. They get you to start exploring the fretboard. A big part of playing **by ear** is being thoroughly familiar with the sounds of your banjo.

I have tabbed out a handful of my favorite **G** and **C** licks for you to experiment with. Do not think that these are the only licks available. Take some of the ideas presented here and play around with them. Start exploring and find your own voice on the banjo.

G licks

Simple G backup
a great little backup lick that I use a lot when I'm singing.

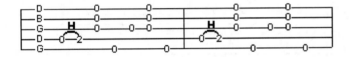

Simple G backup 2
this time with a phantom **hammer-on**.

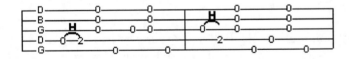

Slide Lick
this one can be tricky at first because it's not exactly an "old time" lick. I picked this one up from a buddy who plays bluegrass banjo. The first measure is two eighth notes, a quarter note and a **bump dit-ty**.

Cascade Lick

If you have to run an open **G** chord for a few measures this lick really makes things more interesting.

Double Slide

If you can **slide** in one direction why not the other?
Hit the string and then **slide** down one fret and back up in one smooth motion.

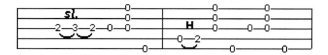

Foggy Mountain Lick

It's not just for bluegrass!

G Tag

This works well in tunes like "**Cripple Creek**." The **pull-off** and **phantom hammer-on** together might take a little bit of work but it is a really cool effect.

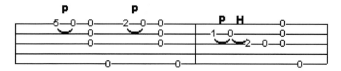

High G

Take a look at your chord chart and you'll see that you have more than one **G** chord on the fretboard. We will be using this same lick in the "Playing Up The Neck" chapter later on.

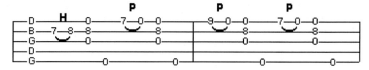

C Licks

Simple C lick

C Pull-off Lick

Back & Forth Lick

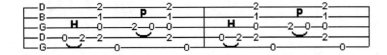

Back & Forth Lick #2

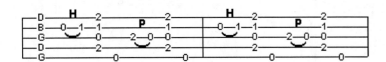

Pinky Lick

This might be a tough one but it is kind of important.
In this lick you are holding a full **C** chord and using your
little finger to **hammer-on** the fourth string at the third fret.
You will have to train your fingers to get this one smooth.

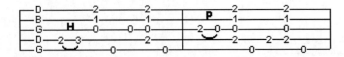

C Tag

Another thing you can try for a **C** lick is
to make a bar chord at the fifth fret
with your index finger and play any of your **G** licks.
If you do the same thing at the *seventh* fret you'll be playing **D** licks. Try it!

Other Licks

All of the **G** and **C** licks we just went through can be adapted to work with any chord form.
Here are a few examples from other chord forms to experiment with.

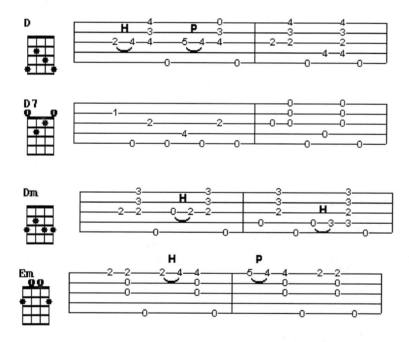

If you look at all of these licks you will see that they are just variations of the basic **bump dit-ty** strum. The melody of the licks is just a result of moving one or two fingers. If you keep these things in mind you will be able to come up with an almost endless variety of sounds that can be used to enhance your playing & singing.

Harmonics

Harmonics or "chimes" are loud resonant notes made by lightly touching a string just over the fifth, seventh or twelfth fret. The trick is that when I say lightly I mean *lightly* touch the string. You don't want to put much pressure on the string. Just touch it directly over the fret.

You can use **harmonics** as single notes or as bar chords. If you make a bar chord harmonic over the fifth fret it is essentially a **C** chord. Over the seventh gives you a **D** chord and at the twelfth…. (remember our bar chord chart?) Right again! You get a **G** chord.

One thing to keep in mind is that with your fifth string being shorter each harmonic note on the fifth string is five frets below the other strings. Just touch the fifth string over the tenth, twelfth and seventeenth fret for your fifth string **harmonics**.

In the "useless but kind of cool in a twisted sort of way" category of banjo tricks you can use **harmonics** to play entire melodies if you wish. To get notes outside of your **C**, **D** and **G** chords you will have to use both hands on the fretboard. This is hard to do but not impossible. You will have to practice fretting a **harmonic** note with the index or middle finger of your picking hand while your thumb plucks the string. Once you can do that you can fret with your left hand using the idea that if your open string has **harmonics** on the fifth, seventh and twelfth frets everything would move one fret down (6, 8 & 9) if you fretted the string at the first fret.

Where you take this idea is up to you. You could go completely crazy and start experimenting with Van Halen style two-handed wire tapping with this if you really wanted to.

Scales

Believe it or not you began working with **scales** as soon as you started tuning your banjo. The key of **G** (your main "banjo key") is based on the **G scale**. When you started playing melody in the keys of **G** and **C** your melody notes fell respectively into the **G and C scales**.

Before we get too deep into what scales are go back and take a look at the <u>G position chord chart</u>. We start with open **G**. When we bar across the first fret we get an **A flat** chord. If we keep moving along the fretboard we wind up with another **G** chord at the twelfth fret. The pattern that is being played out here is a big part of understanding how music works.

Right about now I should mention that I picked this concept up on a gig with a Philadelphia string band (Mummers) in the pouring rain from a banjo player in a clown suit who was just about three sheets to the wind.

I did take some music theory classes in college but to be perfectly honest the guy in the clown suit did a better job of explaining this than my professor ever did.

Where was I?

Oh yeah, music theory. In Western music (and when I say "Western" I don't mean cowboy music. It refers to *Western civilization*. In Asian cultures they have a slightly different set of rules, which is why Indian and Chinese music sounds so exotic to our ears) there are twelve different notes. The twelve notes are named after the letters **A** through **G** with a note or *half-step* between each pair of letters except between **B** and **C** and **E** and **F**:

A | B C | D | E F | G |

Your half step is either a **sharp (#)** or a **flat (b.)**

The half step between **A** and **B** can be called either **A#** or **Bb**.

A# means that the **A** note is *raised* one half step higher. **Bb** is the **B** note *lowered* one half step. **A#** and **Bb** are the same note and the other half steps follow the same pattern.

So with all twelve notes laid out you have the chromatic scale:

A	A#/Bb	B	C	C#/Db	D	D#/Eb	E	F	F#/Gb	G	G#/Ab
1	2	3	4	5	6	7	8	9	10	11	12

Once you understand the idea of half steps you can just write out your chromatic scale like this to save space and make it a tad clearer.

The " | " symbol will be used to represent a half step.

A | B C | D | E F | G |

To hear this on your banjo play the third string at the second fret (an **A** note) and play that string on each fret all the way through twelve frets for each note of the chromatic scale.

When a song is in the key of **G** it means that the song is played out of the **G** scale. Actually the technical term is something like "the key of **G** is a major mode with a root of "**G**" but talking that way makes my brain hurt. We are not going to get into modes just yet.

To figure out the notes of the **G scale** we need to lay out the string of notes starting with our *root note*. In this case the root note is **G**:

G | A | B C | D | E F | G

Now if you notice we started on **G** and ended on **G**. That second **G** is called the **octave**. It is the same note as the root but higher in pitch. If we wrote this out to work the **C** scale it would look like this with **C** as the root note:

C | D | E F | G | A | B C

What we have here is a chromatic scale starting on **G** and ending on **G** and a second scale in **C**. In order to make the first one a **G** major scale we need to pick seven notes out of the twelve notes in the chromatic scale. In order to do that we just follow a simple formula:

Root, whole step, whole step, half step, whole step, whole step, whole step, half step

G is the root.

1. a <u>whole step</u> from **G** is **A**.
2. a <u>whole step</u> from **A** is **B**.
3. a *half step* from **B** is **C**
4. a <u>whole step</u> from **C** is **D**
5. a <u>whole step</u> from **D** is **E**
6. a <u>whole step</u> from **E** is. . .**F#** or **Gb**. We'll call it **F#**
7. a *half step* from **F#** is **G** which gives you the **octave**.

So your **G** scale is
G A B C D E F# G
Lets try to figure out a **C** scale.

Lay out the **chromatic** scale.

C | D | E F | G | A | B C

Follow the pattern of whole steps & half steps:

Root, whole step, whole step, half step, whole step, whole step, whole step, half step

And our **C** scale is
C D E F G A B C

You can follow these steps to find the other major scales on your own.

Now this stuff is really nifty to know but I am pretty sure that right about now you are thinking, "How is this going to help me play the banjo?"

Well it helps in a couple of ways. First, almost every melody line that you are going to play in a major key falls into a major scale. Being able to use scales in your banjo playing will let you come up with melody lines and variations of melody lines without any real effort.

For example, take a look at this **G** scale. Now go back and look at the tab for the songs we have worked on in the key of **G**.

```
D-------------------------0--2--4--5-------
B-------------------0--1-------------------
G----------0--2---------------------------
D-----------------------------------------
G-----------------------------------------
```

Do you see the pattern?

By taking the time to find other **G** scales on the fretboard you really can open up an endless well of possibilities.

It is easy to find a scale on the fretboard. Pick a note and follow the series of whole steps and half steps that we used to work out the **G** and **C** scales:

Root, whole step, whole step, half step, whole step, whole step, whole step, half step

Just keep in mind that a whole step on the banjo fretboard is two frets. A half step is one fret.

As for what note to start on, well you already know that.

Here are the first twelve notes on the first string:

D, D#/Eb, E, F, F#/Gb, G, G#/Ab, A, A#/Bb, B, C, C#/Db

As you can see this is just the chromatic scale starting on a **D** note because . . .you guessed it. The first string is tuned to **D**. I'll let you figure out the other strings on your own.

Another cool thing you can do with scales is to use **The Nashville Number System** to figure out chord progressions.

The Nashville Number System

The Nashville Number System is a trick that musicians use to figure out chord progressions on the fly. It is an easy tool to use if you understand how music works. It has been around for about four hundred years but sometime during the past fifty years Nashville got the credit.

The **Nashville Number System** uses major scales to figure out which chords to play in a given key. This is useful in two ways. In one application you can use the number system to figure out a chord progression as you are playing the song.

Another way to use the number system is to figure out how to play a song in a different key. This is called *transposing* a song.

You start out by writing down a scale, in this case **G** major. Then number each note.

1 2 3 4 5 6 7 8

G A B C D E F# G

The notes numbered **1**, **4** and **5** (**G**, **C** and **D**) will be your major chords for the key of **G**.

Go back and look at all the songs in the key of **G** that we covered earlier. You will notice that almost all of them use some combination of **G**, **C** and **D**. Some songs will only have two of the chords but most of the time you will see all three.

The note numbered **6** is going to be your *relative minor*. In this case **Em**.

Every root chord has a relative minor chord. I do not want to go too deep into music theory here but every major key has a unique number of sharps and flats. The key of **C** has no sharps or flats and the key of **G** has one sharp (**F#**.) The same rule applies to minor keys. Any minor key that has the same number of sharps and flats as a major key is the relative minor of that major key.

The key of **Am** has no sharps or flats. Therefore it is the relative minor of **C**.

The key of **Em** has one sharp so it is the relative minor of **G**.

It is good to know your relative minor chords (the **6** chord in the number system) because you can swap them around in some situations. If you are playing a song and cannot remember how to make an **Am** chord you can just play a **C** chord. It *is* different but it is close enough that you may get away with it.

The note numbered **2** is going to be both a minor chord *and* a major chord.
In this case **Am** and **A**.

Number **3** is where it gets kind of neat because in folk music this is often referred to as an "off chord." In the key of **G** your off chord is **B**.

Your **6** chord can be played as a major chord as well. But it is kind of funky. You will really only use the major **6** once in a great while. An example of the **6** chord in action can be found in **"Salty Dog."**

In some songs like **"Little Maggie"** you might run into what some players call a mountain seven. That is when you flat the **7** chord. That is why **"Little Maggie"** goes from **G** to **F** rather than **G** to **F#**.

The important thing to remember is **1- 4- 5**. That is the way to find the three most commonly used chords in any key. Don't go all goofy with this and start yammering about **2** chords at a jam. **The Nashville Number System** is great but it is just a tool. Simply knowing the chord progression is not enough. In the next chapter we will explain how to *use* chord progressions.

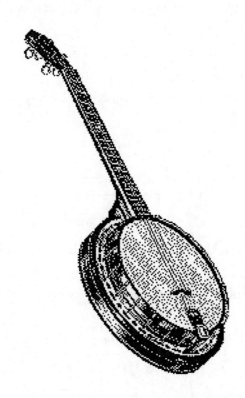

Getting The Feel of The Music

A big part of playing by ear is getting used to how a chord progression *feels*. This is pretty hard to write about because there is no particular technique involved.

When you go to a jam session and the group starts playing a song that you do not know you can use the **Nashville Number System** to get an idea of the chord progression. However actually playing the song involves being able to work with those chords. It is not a matter of thinking "Ok, a **G** chord goes here." It's a bit more intuitive than that.

Let's play a song in the key of **G**. The chorus of "**Will The Circle Be Unbroken**" is a good one for this because just about everyone has heard it. The song is in 4/4 time.

> **Will the circle be unbroken?**
> **By and by lord, by and by**
> **There's a better home a waiting**
> **In the sky Lord in the sky**

Now we know our **1- 4- 5 progression** for the Key of **G** is **G**, **C** and **D**. So let's try the first line of "**Will The Circle Be Unbroken**" with a **G** chord. We know that it is in 4/4 time so let's just play an open **G bump dit-ty** and sing:

G

Will the circle be unbroken?   By and by lord, by and by

When you just hold the **G** chord through the first line you will get this funny feeling that something is not right. It feels like there a chord change somewhere that we are missing.

G

Will the circle be unbroken?   By and **by** lord, by and by

Right where the verse goes to "By and **by**" there is a chord change. The question is what chord do we change to?

Well you have two choices. We know it's not **G** so it must be either **C** or **D**.
Let's try going to **D**:

G   **D**

Will the circle be unbroken?   By and **by** lord, by and by

How does that feel?   Kind of *wrong*, right?

So let's try it with a **C** chord:

G   **C**

Will the circle be unbroken?   By and **by** lord, by and by

Makes a big difference doesn't it?

Now go through the rest of the tune on your own. I will mark out the places where the chords change but it is up to you to figure out what chord to change to.

```
G                          C
```
Will the circle be unbroken?   By and **by** lord, bye and **by**

There's a better home a waiting in the sky Lord **in** the **sky**.

One thing to keep in mind is that more often than not a song ends with the same chord that it began with. So on the "in" we're either going to **C** or **D** then back to **G** at "sky."

I'll write out the other verses for you and mark out the chord changes from the first verse.

"Will The Circle Be Unbroken"

> **I was standing by my window**
> **On a cold & cloudy day.**
> **When I saw that hearse come rolling**
> **For to carry my mother away.**
>
> *Chorus:*
> **Will the circle be unbroken?**
> **By and by, Lord by and by.**
> **There's a better home a waiting**
> **In the sky, Lord in the sky.**
>
> **Lord, I told that undertaker**
> **"Undertaker please drive slow**
> **For this body you are hauling,**
> **Lord, I hate to see her go."**
>
> **Well I followed close behind her**
> **Tried to hold up and be brave.**
> **But I could not hide my sorrow**
> **As they laid her in her grave.**

The only way this ever seems to really sink in is to play a lot of songs. The more songs you play and sing the easier it is to see how chords and chord progressions interact with each other.

In the following pages I have provided the lyrics and chord progressions for a handful of songs. Run through them with your basic frailing strum and sing the lyrics. Find three or four that you really like and just play them constantly for a few days. Then pick another three songs. It may be a little tricky at first to figure out the song if you have never heard it but if you look at the lyrics there is a certain kind of poetry to them. Spend some time singing the lyrics while strumming and changing chords. After a while it all just makes sense.

If you really want a recorded version of a tune there is an almost limitless number of resources. Check your local library for recordings. Ask a musician friend to help you. Bug your local radio stations to start playing more folk music. Surf the Internet. Sites like http://www.mudcat.org and http://www.honkingduck.com have an amazing number of free sound files to work with. Look around and see what you can find.

Don't think you are limited to these tunes. Pick up a copy of <u>Rise Up Singing,</u> <u>The Folksingers' Wordbook</u> or any other songbook. Then play anything and everything that catches your fancy. The important thing is to start working on getting the feel of a chord progression. When you are not practicing listen to recordings and see if you can spot where chords change in the song.

Once you can play these songs in a particular key go back and use the
Nashville Number System to play them in a different key.

1 2 3 4 5 6 7 8

G A B C D E F# G   The 1-4-5 progression for the key of **G** is G, C & D

1 2 3 4 5 6 7 8

C D E F G A B C   The 1-4-5 progression for the key of **C** is C, F & G

1 2 3 4 5 6 7 8

D E F# G A B C# D The 1-4-5 progression for the key of **D** is D, G & A

You can work out other keys on your own.
Have fun and don't forget to sing!

"Mamma Don't 'low"
4/4 Time Key of G
G
Mamma don't 'low no
G
Banjo playin' round here
G
Mamma don't 'low no
D7
banjo playin' round here
       G
Well, I don't care what
G
mamma don't 'low
         C
Gonna play banjo anyhow
 G
Mamma don't 'low no
D7   G
banjo playin' round here

Mamma don't low no
cussin' and swearin' 'round here etc.

Mamma don't low no
guitar playin' round here etc.

"Riley The Furniture Man"
4/4 Time Key of G
G
When I was a poor boy, oh so sad
           C
That Riley from Virginia took
           G
Everything I had

Chorus:
G
Riley's been here
D7   G
got my furniture and gone!

Now it makes no difference to a rich man
with all his fancy clothes
if you don't pay Mr. Riley
you got no place to go.

Riley come to my house
and these are the words he said
throw that cracker driver out
and load that poster bed.

Now Riley he's a rich man
off poor folks like me
every Sunday morning Riley
gives to charity.

"The Rambles Of Spring"
4/4 Time Key of G

G
There's a fierce and wintry breeze
          C   G
blowing through the budding tress
                                  D7
and I button up my coat to keep me warm
         G
but the days are on the mend
        C   G
and I'm heading home again
                    D7
G
with me fiddle snuggled close beneath me
arm

chorus:
G   C   D7
I've a fine felt hat and a strong pair of
brogues
          G   D7
I've got rosin in my pocket for me bow
G
and my fiddle strings are new
C
and I've learned a tune or two
      G   D7   G
so I'm well prepared to ramble and must go

I'm as happy as a king
when I catch a breath of Spring
and the grass is turning green as Winter
ends
And the geese are on the wing
and the thrushes start to sing
and I'm traveling down the road
to meet my friends

Here's a health to one and all
to you big and to you small
to rich & poor alike and foe and friend
Until we return again
may your foe be turned to friend
and may peace and joy be with you until
then.

"Sailor On The Deep Blue Sea"
4/4 Time Key Of G

G   C
It was on one summer's evening
G   D7
Just about the hour of three
             G   C
When my darling started to leave me
             G   D7   G
For to sail upon the deep blue sea

Oh he promised to write me a letter
He said he's write to me
But I have not heard from my darling
Who is sailing on the deep blue sea

Oh captain can you tell me
Where can my sailor be?
Oh yes little maiden
he is drowned in the deep blue sea

Farewell to friends and relations
it's the last you'll see of me
I'm going to end my troubles
by drowning in the deep blue sea

"Roll In My Sweet Baby's Arms"
4/4 Time Key of G

G
Ain't gonna work on the railroad
                                D7
Ain't gonna work on the farm
G
lay 'round this shack till the
C
mail train comes back
          G   D7   G
And I'll roll in my sweet baby's arms.

Chorus:
Roll in my sweet baby's arms
Roll in my sweet baby's arms
I'll lay 'round this shack
till the mail train comes back
And I'll roll in my sweet baby's arms.

Sometimes there's a
change in the ocean
Sometimes there's a
change in the sea
Sometimes there's a
change in my own true love
But there ain't no change in me

"Rosewood Casket"
4/4 Time Key of G

```
G              C  D7   G
There's a little rosewood casket
G              C  D7 G
Sitting on a marble stand
           C        G
And a packet of love letters
     D7                  G
written in my true love's hand
```

Come and read them to me, sister
come and sit beside my bed
lay your head upon my pillow
for tomorrow I'll be dead

When I'm dead and in my coffin
and my shroud's around me bound
and my narrow grave is ready
in some lonesome churchyard ground

"The Sweet Sunny South"
4/4 Time Key Of G

```
G
Take me back to the place
                   D7
where I first saw the light
       G                    C
to the sweet sunny South take me home
        G          C
where the mockingbird sings me
     G        D7
to sleep every night
     G        D7      G
oh why was I tempted to roam?
```

I think with regret of the dear ones I left
of the warm hearts that sheltered me then
of the wife and the family of whom I'm bereft
for the old place again I do sigh

Take me back let me see what is left that I
knew
can it be that the old place is gone?
Dear friends from my childhood
indeed must be few
and I must face death all alone

"The Wabash Cannonball"
4/4 Time Key of G

```
G
From the great Atlantic Ocean
                    C
to the wide Pacific Shore
               D
From the Queen of flowing mountains
                        G
to the South Belle by the door
G
She's long and tall and handsome
                        C
well known by one and all
         D
She's a modern combination
                        G
called the Wabash Cannonball
```

Chorus:
```
G
Listen to the jingle
                   C
The rumble and the roar
D
riding through the woodlands
                     G
to the hill and by the shore.
G
Hear the might rush of engines
                        C
hear the lonesome hobo squall
D
riding though the jungles on
                        G
the Wabash Cannonball
```

The Eastern states are dandies
so the Western people say
from New York to St. Louis
and Chicago by the way
through the hills of Minnesota
where the rippling waters fall
no chances need be taken on
the Wabash Cannonball

Here's to Daddy Claxton
may his name forever stand
he will always be remembered
by the 'boes throughout our land
his earthly race is over and
the curtain 'round him falls
we'll carry him to victory on
the Wabash Cannonball

"The Titanic"

4/4 Time Key of G

G
Oh they built the ship Titanic
    C   G
to sail the ocean blue
G
and they thought they had a ship
        A   D
that the water would never go through
       G
but the Lord's almighty hand said that
C
ship would never land
     G
it was sad when that
D   G
great ship went down

chorus:
C   G
It was sad, it was sad
G
it was sad when that
b
great ship went down
G
husbands and wives
C
little children lost their lives
      G
it was sad when that
D   G
great ship went down

Oh they left the coast of England
a thousand miles from shore
when the rich refused to associate
with the poor
so they put them down below
where they'd be the first to go
it was sad when that
great ship went down

They swung the lifeboats out
o'er the cruel and raging sea
when the band struck up with
"nearer my God to thee"
Little children wept and cried
and the waves swept over the side
it was sad when that great ship went down

"Shady Grove"

4/4 Time Key of Em

Em   D
Cheeks as red as a blooming rose
Em
eyes of the prettiest brown
G   D
she's the darling of my heart
         Em
prettiest girl in town

Chorus:
Shady Grove my little love
Shady Grove my darling
Shady Grove my little love
I'm bound for Shady Grove

I went to see my Shady Grove
she was standing by the door
shoes and stockings in her had
little bare feet on the floor

I wish I had a big fine horse
and corn to feed him on
a pretty little girl to stay at home
feed him when I'm gone

"Looking Out A Window"

4/4 Time Key of G

G
 While looking out a window
G
a second story window
                                 D
I fell and broke my eyelash on the pavement
G
go get the Listerine
C
sister wants a beau
        G   D   G
and a boy's best friend is his mother!

They spanked him with a shingle
which made his panties tingle
because he went and socked his little
brother
we feed the baby garlic
so we can find him in the dark
and a boy's best friend is his mother!

Looking through the knothole
in grandpa's wooden leg
who will bring the cows in when I'm gone?
go get the axe there's a flea on Nellie's ear
and a boy's best friend is his mother!

"Over the Mountain"
3/4 Time Key of G
G   C
I'm always light-hearted and easy,
    G   D
Not a care in this world have I,
    G   C
Because I am loved by somebody,
        G   D   G
Who's sitting home waiting for me.

Chorus:
C   G
She's over, just over the mountains,
                     D
Where the little birds sing on the trees,
    G   C
In a cabin all covered in ivy,
    G   D   G
somebody is waiting for me.

She lives far away on the mountains,
Where the little birds sings on the trees,
And the cabin's all covered in ivy,
And somebody is waiting for me.

"Salty Dog"
4/4 Time Key of G
G   E
Let me be your salty dog
  A
or I won't be your man at all
G   D   G
honey let me be your salty dog

Sitting on the corner
with the low down blues
a great big hole in my new shoes
honey let me be your salty dog

I pulled the trigger
and the gun said go
You could hear it way down in Mexico
honey let me be your salty dog

"The Billboard Song"
4/4 Time Key of G
G
As I was walking down the street
                   D
one dark and dusky day
D
I came a across a billboard
                G
with pieces blown away
 G
it was all torn and tattered
                  C
from a storm the night before
    G   D   G
and reading all the pieces this is what I saw

Smoke Coca-Cola cigarettes
chew Wrigley's Spearmint beer
Ken-L-Ration dog food
will make your complexion clear
doctors say that babies
should smoke until their three
and people over 65
should bathe in Lipton's Tea.

Enjoy your next vacation
in a band new Fridgidare
learn to play the piano
in your thermal underwear
if you want to make your country
a better place today
buy a record of this song
and break it right away!

"The Black Velvet Band"
3/4 Time Key of G

G
Her eyes they shone like the diamonds
                            D
you'd think she was queen of the land
G   Em
with her hair hung over her shoulder
     C   D   G
tied up with a black velvet band

As I went walking one morning
not meaning to stray very far
I met with a frolicsome damsel
plying her trade at the bar

A watch she pulled from her pocket
and slipped it right into my hand
on the very first day that I met her
bad luck to the black velvet band

Before judge and jury next morning
I was called out to appear
a gentleman claimed his jewelry
and the case against me was quite clear

Seven long years transportation
right down to "Van Dieman's land"
far away from my friends and companions
to follow the black velvet band

"Railroad Bill"
4/4 Time Key of G

G
Railroad Bill, Railroad Bill
B   C
he never worked and he never will
       G   D   G
and it's ride old Railroad Bill

Railroad Bill was a mighty mean man
he shot the midnight lantern out
the breakman's hand
and it's ride old Railroad Bill

I've got a 38 special on a 45 frame
how can I miss when I've got dead aim?
and it's ride old Railroad Bill

Going up a mountain going out west
38 special sticking out my vest
and it's ride old Railroad Bill

"Oh, Susanna"
4/4 Time Key of G

G
I come from Alabama
                    D
with a banjo on my knee
G
I'm going to Lou'siana
             D   G
my true love for to see
G
It rained all night the day I left
                        D
the weather it was dry
G
The sun so hot I froze to death
          D   G
Susanna don't you cry

Chorus:
C   G   D
Oh, Susanna, don't you cry for me
G
I come from Alabama with
          D   G
my banjo on my knee

I had a dream the other night
when everything was still
I dreamed I saw Susanna
A-coming down the hill

A red rose was in her cheek
A tear was in her eye
I said to her Susanna girl
Susanna don't you cry.

"Corrina, Corrina"
4/4 Time Key of G
G
Corrina, Corrina
D   G
where you been so long?
G
Corrina, Corrina
C   G
Where you been so long?
          D
Ain't had no loving
              G
Since you've been gone.

I've got a bird that whistles
I've got a bird that sings (2x)
If I ain't got Corrina
I ain't got a thing

I'd cross the ocean
on the bottom of the sea (2x)
Because I can't breathe
when she talks to me

"Shenandoah"
4/4 Time Key of C
C   F   C
Oh Shenandoah, I long to see you
F   C
away you rolling river
Am   G   Am
Oh Shenandoah, I long to see you
C   F   C
Away, we're bound away
        Am G   C
Cross the wide Missouri

For seven years I've been a rover
Away you rolling river
For seven years I've been a rover
Away, we're bound away
'cross the wide Missouri

Oh Shenandoah I love your daughter
Away your rolling river
Oh Shenandoah I love your daughter
Away, we're bound away
'cross the wide Missouri

"Drunken Sailor"
4/4 Time Key of Em
Em
What shall we do with a drunken sailor?
D
What shall we do with a drunken sailor?
Em
What shall we do with a drunken sailor?
Em D   Em
Early in the morning

Chorus:
Way hey up she rises (3x)
Early in the morning

Shave his belly with a rusty razor (3x)
Early in the morning

Put him in the longboat till he's sober (3x)
Early in the morning

Put him in the suppers with a
hose pipe on him (3x)
Early in the morning

Heave him by the leg in a running bowline
(3x)
Early in the morning

"Careless Love"
4/4 Time Key of G
G   D   G
Love, oh love oh careless love
G   D
Love, oh love oh careless love
G   B   C
Love, oh love oh careless love
           G   D   G
you can see what careless love has done

I love my momma and poppa too (3x)
But I'd leave them both to go with you

When I wore my apron low (3x)
You'd walk to me through rain and snow

Now I wear my apron high (3x)
You pass my gate and walk on by

You might get by my garden gate (3x)
But you won't get by my .38

"Sweet Betsy From Pike"
3/4 Time Key of C

```
C                                    G
C
Did you ever hear tell of sweet Betsy from
Pike
                                     G
who crossed the wide prairie with her lover
Ike
         F            C          F         C
With two yoke of oxen and an old yellow
dog
                            G           C
A tall Shanghai rooster and a one spotted
hog
```
Chorus:
```
C                         G
Singing toora la roolah la roola la la
```

One evening quite early they camped
on the Platte
'twas near by the road on a green shady flat
where Betsy sore footed lay down to repose
while Ike gazed with wonder on
that Pike County rose

They stopped at Salt Lake to inquire the
way
when Bringham declared that Betsy should
stay
But Betsy got frightened and ran like a deer
while Bringham stood pawing the
ground like a steer

Long Ike and sweet Betsy attended a dance
Ike wore a pair of his Pike county pants
Sweet betsy was covered with ribbons and
rings
says Ike "You're an angel but
where are your wings?"

"The Streets of Laredo"
3/4 Time Key of C

```
C           F        C        G
As I walked out in the streets of Laredo
C           F        C        G
As I walked out in Laredo one day
 C                  F              C
G
I spied a poor cowboy all wrapped in white
linen
        C              F      G         G
all wrapped in white linen as cold as the
clay
```

"I can see by your outfit that you are a
cowboy"
these words he did say as I proudly stepped
by
"Come sit down beside me
and hear my sad story,
got shot in the breast and I know I must
die."

'twas one in the saddle I used to go roaming
'twas once in the saddle I used to go gay
'twas first to the drinking
and then the card playing.
Got shot in the breast and I'm dying today."

"Let six jolly cowboys come carry my coffin.
Let six pretty girls come carry my pall.
Throw bunches of roses all over my coffin
throw roses to deaden the clods as they
fall."

"Oh beat the drum slowly and play the fife
lowly
and play the dead march as you carry me
along.
Take me to the green valley and
lay the earth o'er me
for I'm a poor cowboy and I know
I've done wrong."

Oh we beat the drum slowly
and played the fife lowly
and bitterly wept as we carried him along
for we all loved out comrade
so brave, young and handsome
we all loved out comrade
although he'd done wrong.

Playing Up The Neck

As I mentioned before you can use scales to play a melody line in more than one place on the fretboard. What we are going to do now is work up a couple of versions of "**Sugar Hill**" to illustrate this concept.

Earlier we went through a basic version of "**Sugar Hill**." It was just an open **G** chord and an **Em** chord played with the basic strum:

"Sugar Hill"
4/4 Time Key of G

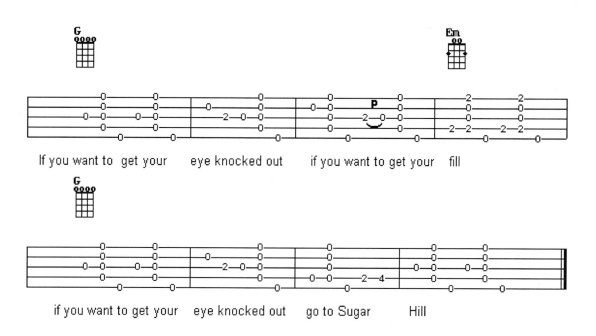

In order to move this up the neck we will use a different **G** and **Em** chord and work our **G** scale out of this new position.

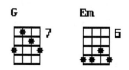

Back in the scales chapter I gave you the tab for a simple **G** scale:

```
 D
 B              0—1    0—2—4—5
 G      0—2
 D
 G
```

In order to move "**Sugar Hill**" up the neck we will need to find a **G** scale near the seventh fret. Remember how we went through this in the chapter on scales. Find the root note and follow the series of whole steps and half steps up, down or across the fretboard. If we do this we will find a **G** scale starting on the fourth string at the fifth fret:

```
D------------------------------
B--------------------7--8------
G-----------------7--9---------
D------5--7--9--10-------------
G------------------------------
```

That will work but something could be a little bit easier. Take a look at the first note of this second **G** scale. It's the same note as your open **third string**. That means you could play the scale like this:

```
D------------------------------
B--------------------7--8------
G------0----------7--9---------
D---------7--9--10-------------
G------------------------------
```

Pretty cool isn't it?

Now for some songs you will need a few higher pitched notes so it might be good to keep this scale going through another octave:

```
D---------------------7--9--10--12----14--16--17------
B-------------------7--8------------------------------
G------0---------7--9---------------------------------
D---------7--9--10------------------------------------
G----------------------------------------------------
```

And let's not forget that the first **G** scale we worked out in the **open G** position can be dragged to the twelfth fret:

```
D----------------12--14--16--17------
B------------12--13------------------
G------12--14------------------------
D-----------------------------------
G-----------------------------------
```

Now if we look at the **C** position **G** chord at the ninth fret and then at the scales we have available it is not too hard to see that a melody line can be worked out around these chord positions just by moving a finger or two.

Before we get into playing a melody line out of this position you have to spend a little time getting used to playing the rhythm with a different set of chord forms. Use the chord diagrams on the bottom of page 87 and just play either your basic strum or a chop while you sing the lyrics.

Once you can do that without muffling the chords give the melody line a shot. I have tabbed out two alternate versions of "**Sugar Hill**" for you.

Both of these alternate arrangements of "**Sugar Hill**" employ a guitar trick called **floating**. **Floating** is when you play a single note up the neck against open strings.

The other thing to keep in mind with both of these alternate arrangements is that your right hand is still doing the same old **bump dit-ty** picking pattern. No matter how advanced you get with your left (fretting) hand the right (picking) hand is still doing the same basic technique that you started with.

"Sugar Hill"
Key of G 4/4 Time

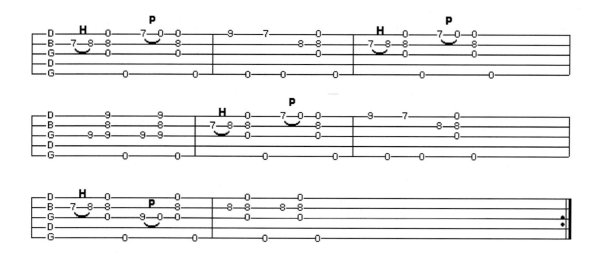

Take a look at this arrangement. See if you can spot how the melody line is pulled out of the scale.

Here's the same song played on different strings. I really like the jump from the higher pitched **G** to the low pitched **Em** chord in this one.

"Sugar Hill"
4/4 Time Key of G

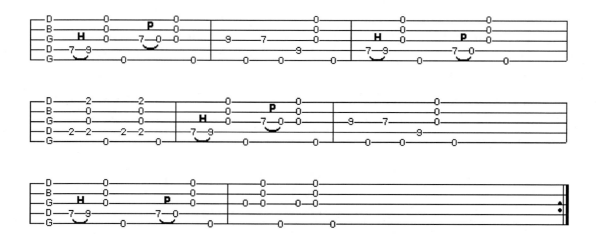

A good way to get used to this concept is to take a bunch of songs you already know and move them into this new position. Start with "**Cripple Creek**" or "**Little Maggie**" and then try looking for other places to work out melody lines.

Chord "Bouncing"

Another great rhythm trick is something I picked up from an old blues guitar player on a subway platform in Philadelphia. He called it "**bouncing**" a chord. This is a fairly simple technique that can add a whole new dimension to your playing. While most of the techniques that we discussed earlier covered breaking up the quarter note in the **bump dit-ty**, bouncing breaks up the strum.

The easiest chord form to "**bounce**" is a bar chord. Most of the time a bar chord is made just by laying one finger across a fret but if you want to **bounce** a chord you have to use *two* fingers.

Let's say we want to **bounce** an **A** chord. Traditionally you just lay your middle finger across the second fret. In this case we are going to do that but we are also going to lay our index finger across the first fret. For a simple **A** chord **bounce** just strum the chord barred at the first fret (an **Ab**) and then **hammer-on** with your middle finger across the second fret.

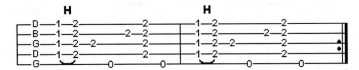

This is fairly easy to do but it can add a lot of spice to a simple solo or back-up arrangement. Try this with your **C** chord at the fifth fret and your **D** chord at the seventh fret.

You can **slide** into a bar chord as well but it has a slightly different feel. You will have to decide for yourself what works best for the song that you are playing.

Here are three examples. A **slide** into an **A** chord, a **double bounce** into a **C** chord and a **long slide** from **A** to **D**. Experiment with these ideas and see what you can come up with.

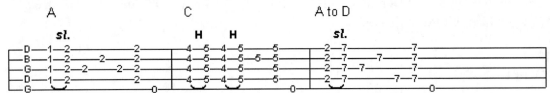

Once you get comfortable **bouncing** bar chords try these ideas with your **C** and **F** position chords. One thing that will make **bouncing** easier, not to mention finding scales and chord progressions, is to get a feel for how the chord positions interact with each other. We'll go over that in the next chapter.

Take another look at how we used the **chop** for the song "**Cripple Creek.**" Try it again but this time **bounce** the chords by starting your **G** chord at the fourth fret and **sliding** it up to the fifth fret. See what you can come up with on your own to **bounce** the **G and C** chords.

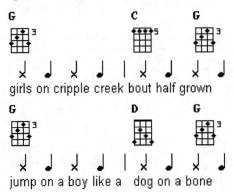

girls on cripple creek bout half grown

jump on a boy like a dog on a bone

Playing In The "Box"

You do not have to jump up and down the fretboard to reach a lot of chords and scales. As you might have noticed in the chapter on playing up the neck a great variety of "stuff" is usually just a fret or two away from wherever you are on the banjo neck.

In this chapter we are going to make some fretboard diagrams to show you how each position has a specific pattern relating to how it interacts with the other chord forms and scales.

Each fretboard diagram shows the five strings of your banjo neck. The lines going down through the strings show the frets. The white dots tell you where to put your fingers.

Nothing to it, right?

Ok, let's look at how the **C position** interacts with the other chord forms.

If you make a **C position** chord anywhere on the fretboard

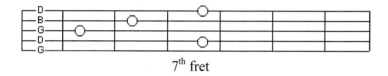

7th fret

You will always have an **F position** chord one fret up the neck

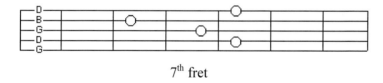

7th fret

And a **G position** chord on the first fret of the **C position** chord

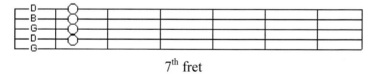

7th fret

This makes sense if you go back and look at how the **C & F** chords relate to each other.

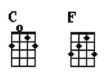

The same rule applies to your **G** and **F positions.**

Anywhere you make a **G position** (or bar) chord:

5th fret

You will always have a **C position** chord starting on the same fret:

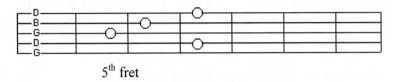

5th fret

And another **C position** chord two frets up:

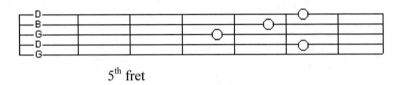

5th fret

And in the **F position** any **F position** chord

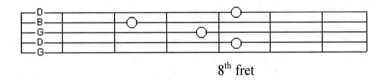

8th fret

Has a **G position** chord on the same fret

8th fret

And a **C** position chord one fret down the neck

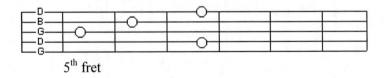

5th fret

Pretty wild isn't it?

Do some exploring on your own and see if you can find any other ways chord forms interact with each other.

Don't forget that your minor chord forms fit into the same kind of patterns.

Your **G** position has a relative minor position

G position:

Relative minor position:

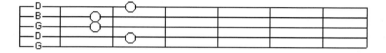

C position:

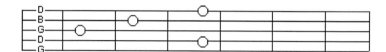

Relative minor position:

F position:

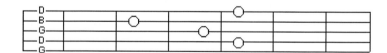

Relative minor position:

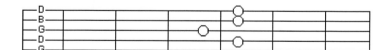

Remember that your relative minor chord is the minor version of the **6** chord in the **Nashville Number System**. What that means is if you make a **G** position **C** chord the relative minor chord in that position will be an **Am** chord. **G** becomes **Em**, **F** becomes **Dm**, **E** becomes **Cm**, **A** becomes **F#m** and so on.

Also be aware that all three of these chord families are within easy reach of several movable scales:

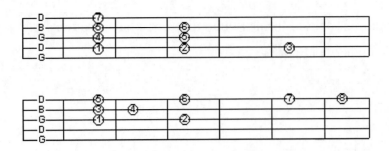

Just follow the numbers in the circles starting with 1 and walk across the fretboard to get your scale.

What all this means is that every chord needed for any chord progression along with at least some part of your major scale (remember that the banjo only has four strings and two of them are tuned to the same note so you cannot get a full scale across a few frets the way you can on the guitar or the mandolin) can be **boxed** into a few frets. Compare what we covered in this chapter to how we arranged "**Sugar Hill**" in the chapter on playing up the neck.

Pinky Power

Playing in the key of **C** out of **G** tuning gets some banjo players confused. It is not that hard a thing to do because you have been playing songs in **C** since the beginning of this book.

That said there is one tricky side to playing in **C** and that is learning to use your little finger to reach some notes.

If you remember back in the chapter on licks we had a deceptively simple little piece of tablature called the "pinky lick":

There is not a whole lot going on in a lick like this but getting your little finger into play can be tricky. In our day-to-day lives we do not use the little finger the same way that we use our ring or index fingers.

There really is no easy or fast way to strengthen your little finger. Some players have gone to extremes trying to develop "pinky power." I used to pile big heavy books on top of my fretting hand and would try to lift them by pressing my fingertips off a tabletop. One of the finest three finger players I have ever known told me once that he used to stick metal pipe fittings on his fingertips and do "pinky curls" like a weight lifter pumping up his biceps. Both of us can tell you from experience that these things will not work. They will, however, do some rather nasty things to your tendons.

So how do we build up some "pinky power?" Well, like I said in the first chapter on setting up your banjo, light gauge strings and a super low action are really important here. The less effort it takes to fret a clean note the easier it will be to build up your fretting hand.

Do not worry about light gauge strings not being loud enough. On a decent banjo with the right set up they can be a lot louder than heavy gauge strings.

After set up the other "secret" ingredient is practice. You will want to add a couple of licks and one or two songs to your daily practice routine and just start to slowly build up strength and flexibility in that fretting hand. Work on getting your little finger as strong and agile as your other digits.

Also start using "full" chords that use all four strings. Hopefully you have already been doing that for at least a little while. If you haven't I suggest that you start.

Make a daily routine of just running your **C**, **F** and **G** chords. You do not have to play a specific song. In fact it would really help your playing by ear skills if you start experimenting with chord progressions. See what chords fit together and just have some fun exploring on your own.

Do that everyday for a few weeks and then add this lick to your practice routine:

This is a **C7** lick. It starts out easy but the two **hammer-on's** in the third measure can be tricky at first. Take this lick nice and slow. Give your fingers time to get used to moving like this.

If you start to feel a lot of tension in your hand or it starts to actually hurt take a break. That whole "feel the burn" routine might work for aerobics but when it comes to playing an instrument it is bad mojo.

If you take a break and it starts to hurt again right away then the odds are you need to look at your hand position. Is your thumb on that imaginary line down the center of the banjo neck? Maybe you have your elbow stuck up in the air rather than in a relaxed position. Analyze what is going on and find a way to correct it.

Give yourself a few weeks to work on that lick. Then add another to your routine.

Just like the last lick this one works out of a **C7** chord. The difference is the **pull-off** and the single string trick in the first measure. The timing in that first measure is two eighth notes, two quarter notes and two eighth notes.

Give yourself some time to work on that and then start experimenting with the first part of **"Home Sweet Home."**

"Home Sweet Home"
4/4 Time Key of **G**

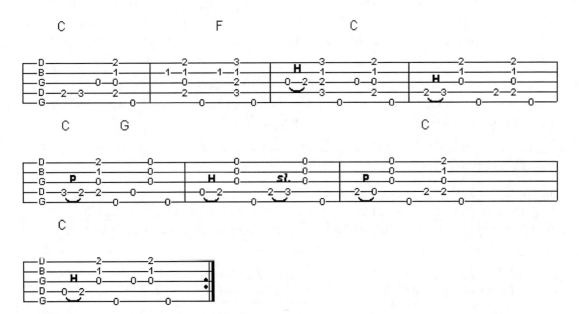

This isn't the whole tune but it is enough for your practice routine.

Once you get comfortable reaching those notes holding a **C** chord move it up the neck and try all of this in the key of **D**.

Give yourself time. If it hurts stop and see what you are doing wrong. Most of all have fun!

Playing In D

While you can get away with using a capo at the second fret and playing out of the **C** position for songs in the key of **D** it is sometimes kind of cool to play in **D** without using a capo.

If we go back to the **Nashville Number System** for the key of **D** we'll find that the 1-4-5 progression for the key of **D** is **D**, **A** and **G**.

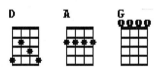

To play melodies in the key of **D** we will also need to work out our **D** scale:

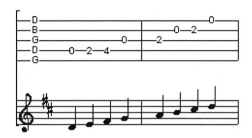

In order to use the scale while holding the **D** chord (you need to hold the chord in order to keep the rhythm going) you will want to take advantage of <u>the two open **D** strings in open **G** tuning.</u>

 If you strum the **D** chord <u>with the first & fourth strings open</u> you not only get a pretty cool drone string effect but you also have two fingers free to work the scale notes.

Now this *is not* a **D** chord but it is close enough to *pass* as a **D** chord as long as you don't use it for more than a couple of measures in row.

This also lets you get away with leaving the first or the fourth string open. This is a real advantage with a chord that uses all four strings because it opens up a lot of neat effects like **hammer-on's** and **pull-off's.** You also might want to try out a few of the **C** licks we discussed earlier in this position. Use the partial **D** chord as a sort of framework to keep the fingering easy.

Before we go on take a little bit of time to play some of the songs we have already gone through in **G** and **C** and use the **Nashville Number System** to play them in **D** with a simple rhythm.

The one tricky part of playing in **D** is the fifth string. Technically the fifth string *should* be tuned up to **A** but the problem here is that with the fifth string tuned to **A** your open **G** chord will not always work and you'll be forced to play an **F** position **G** chord at the fifth fret.

Now that works fine and it is something you should be able to do anyway but in some arrangements that open **G** chord really sounds cool. So if we leave the fifth string tuned to **G** we will have to use a lighter touch with our thumb. You may also wish to mute the fifth string with the heel of your hand occasionally.

Experiment with this and use whatever sounds best to your ears.

Let's play "**Boil Them Cabbage Down**" in **D**. I wrote out a simple version in tab. Once you get comfortable with this start adding some **hammer-on's** and whatnot like we did for the key of **C**.

"Boil Them Cabbage Down"
*4/4 Time Key of **D***

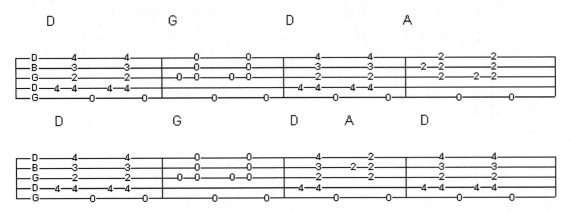

"**Dicey Riley**" is a neat old Irish song. I learned this when I was playing with a band from Belfast. It is one of the first songs I ever worked up in **D**. I had to figure this out on stage in front of a pretty rowdy audience so it always brings back a lot of memories.

"Dicey Riley"
4/4 Time Key of D

She walks along Fitzgibbon Street with an independent air.
And then it's down by Summerhill where the people stop and stare
She says it's nearly half past one and it's time I had another little one
Ah the heart of the poor old Dicey Riley.

"Wind That Shakes The Barley"
4/4 Time key of D

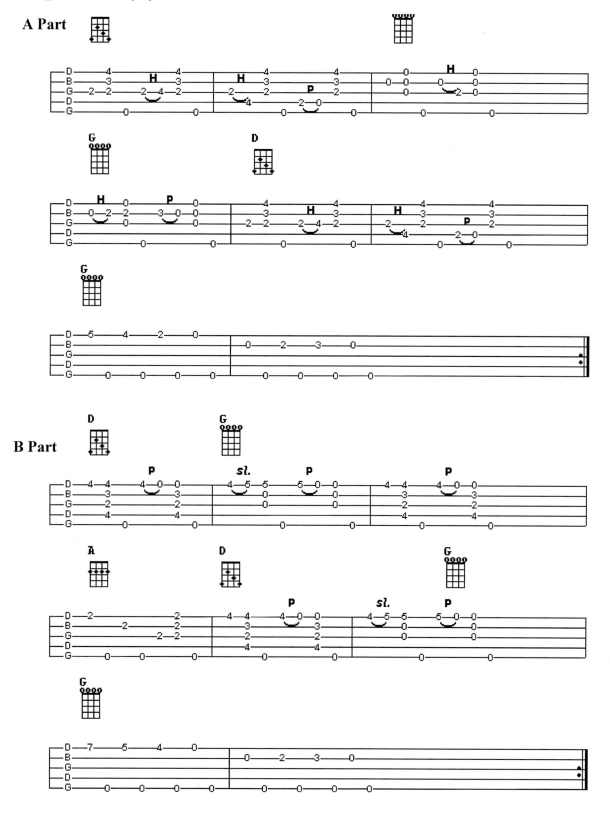

Minor Scales

The crazy thing about minor scales is that there are three different versions of the minor scale: **Natural Minor**, **Harmonic Minor** and **Melodic Minor**.

Natural Minor

The **natural minor scale** is the most common of the three. It works under the same concept as your **major scale** in that you have a root note followed by a series of whole steps and half steps. The difference is in the way the whole steps and half steps are laid out:

> **Root, whole step, half step, whole step, whole step, half step, whole step, whole step.**

To create an **A natural minor scale** the first step is to lay out the A **chromatic scale**:

A| B C | D | E F | G | A

A is the **root**.

- A <u>whole step</u> from **A** is **B**
- A <u>half step</u> from **B** is **C**
- A <u>whole step</u> from **C** is **D**
- A <u>whole step</u> from **D** is **E**
- A <u>half step</u> from **E** is **F**
- A <u>whole step</u> from **F** is **G**
- A <u>whole step</u> from **G** is **A**

So our **A** minor scale is:
A B C D E F G A

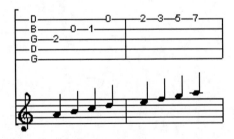

Now you will notice that the **A minor** scale has no sharps or flats. The only major scale with no sharps or flats is the **C major** scale.

Because **A minor** and **C major** have the same number of sharps and flats **A minor** is the **relative minor** of **C**.

Take a look at the **B minor** scale:

The chromatic scale in **B** is:

B C | D | E F | G | A | B

B is the **root**.

- A <u>whole step</u> from **B** is **C#**
- A <u>half step</u> from **C#** is **D**
- A <u>whole step</u> from **D** is **E**
- A <u>whole step</u> from **E** is **F#**
- A <u>half step</u> from **F#** is **G**
- A <u>whole step</u> from **G** is **A**
- A <u>whole step</u> from **A** is **B**

Our **B minor scale** is:

B C# D E F# G A B

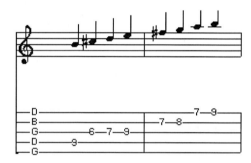

You can see that the **B minor** scale has two sharps--- **C#** and **F#**. This is exactly the same as the key of **D major**. That means **B minor** is the **relative minor** of **D**.

This can be confusing at first because an **A** major scale sounds nothing like a **C** major scale. It is a common mistake to think that **A** and **Am** are somehow related--- after all, both scales start with an **A** note.

Minor scales are actually a **mode** of a major scale. A **mode** is when you play a scale starting with something other than the **root** note. It's a very old concept that was developed back in the Dark Ages for church music.

I know, you didn't expect to be playing stuff from the Spanish Inquisition on your banjo.

Then again, "Nobody expects a Spanish Inquisition!"

I'm sorry. I just couldn't resist that one.

At this point you have been messing around with two modes. **Ionian** and **Aeolian**.

Don't say, "no I haven't" because the **Ionian** mode is what you used to create a major scale and **Aeolian** mode is what you just used to create a minor scale.

Let's take a look at a **C major** scale:

C D E F G A B C

In your major scale or **Ionian mode** you start with the **root** note. We have already covered how to build a major scale so I won't go over that again. Nothing changes.

When we went on to build an **A minor** scale we started with the root note because it's easier. If we were to play the **C** scale in **Aeolian mode** we would start with the sixth note (**A**) of the scale and run through to the next **A**.

So your **C** scale: **C D E F G A B C**

Becomes an Am scale: **A B C D E F G A**

That's why a major scale and its **relative minor** scale share the same number of sharps and flats. C and Am are the same scale in different modes.

Let's try the same thing with **D** and **B minor**:

The **D major scale** (or **D Ionian**): D E F# G A B C# D

D Aeolian (or **B minor**):   B C# D E F# G A B

The scale is named **B minor** but it is more closely related to **D**. Each scale has two sharps. That's why we call **B minor** the relative minor of the key of **D**.

This is easy to remember if you go back to **The Nashville Number System**. The "6 chord" is always your **relative minor**.

The two variations of the **natural minor scale** are technically the same scale with a few small differences that make them sound like totally different scales.

Harmonic Minor

The **harmonic minor** scale is a variation of your **natural minor scale**. Everything stays the same except for the number of steps between the fifth and the sixth notes of the scale.

In the harmonic minor scale you lay out the whole and half steps as:

      Root, whole step, half step, whole step, whole step, half step, whole step plus half, whole step.

To create an **A harmonic minor scale** the first step is to lay out the **A chromatic scale**:

A| B C | D | E F | G | A

A is the **root**.

- A <u>whole step</u> from **A** is **B**
- A <u>half step</u> from **B** is **C**
- A <u>whole step</u> from **C** is **D**
- A <u>whole step</u> from **D** is **E**
- A <u>half step</u> from **E** is **F**
- A <u>whole step</u> from **F** is **G**. *Add one more <u>half step</u> to* **G#**
- A <u>whole step</u> from **G** is **A**

So our **A harmonic minor** scale is:
A B C D E F G# A

Melodic Minor

The **melodic minor scale** is a little bit more unusual. The other scales we have looked at up to now are played the same way *ascending* or *descending* (up or down) the scale.

Melodic minor changes things by having one set of whole and half steps while *ascending* the scale and <u>another set of whole and half steps</u> while *descending* the scale.

The first set (ascending) of whole and half steps in a **melodic minor scale** are:

whole step, half step, whole step, whole step, whole step, whole step, half step.

To create an **A melodic minor scale** we start, as usual, with the chromatic scale:

A| B C | D | E F | G | A

A is the **root**.

- A <u>whole step</u> from **A** is **B**
- A <u>whole step</u> from **B** is **C**
- A <u>whole step</u> from **C** is **D**
- A <u>whole step</u> from **D** is **E**
- A <u>whole step</u> from **E** is **F#**
- A <u>whole step</u> from **F#** is **G#**
- A <u>half step</u> from **G#** is **A**

So the first half, or *ascending section*, of our **A melodic minor** scale is:

A B C D E F# G# A

The *descending* part of the **A melodic minor scale** is easy because it is the same notes we used for the natural minor scale. The only tricky part is that we have to go *backwards* (remember, this is the descending part of the scale.)

A G F E D C B A

So the entire **A melodic minor** scale is:

A B C D E F# G# A G F E C B A

Nine times out of ten all you will really need to use is the natural minor (or **C Aeolian**) scale. The other two scales may come in handy somewhere down the road. Experiment with minor key songs and try using a minor scale to work out the melody line.

Also keep in mind that minor scales can be moved around on the fretboard just as easily as the major scales.

A natural minor

Remember! Even with the added sharps and flats, these **A harmonic** and **A melodic** variations are directly related to the A minor scale.

More Cool Stuff
With Scales & Chords

Now that we are starting to explore the fretboard, it is time we took a quick look at some other things that you can pull out of a scale.

Build your own chords

We have been using major, minor and seventh chords for a good while now without discussing what they are and how they are built. This is not stuff that you *have* to know but you can use it to do some pretty cool stuff.

A chord is made up of a combination of notes from a scale. Remember how to come up with a **G** scale?

G A B C D E F# G

A **major chord** is made up of the 1st, 3rd, 5th notes in the scale.

G A B C D E F# G
1 2 3 4 5 6 7 8

A **G major chord** is made up of the notes **G-B-D**. If you play those three notes together anywhere on the fretboard you are playing a **G major chord**.

If you want to figure out the notes for any major chord, just write out the appropriate scale (to figure out the **G** chord we used a **G** scale) and find the 1st, 3rd and 5th notes in the scale.

A **minor chord** is made up of the same three notes but in a minor chord we flat the third note. That means we lower the pitch of the third note by a half step. So, a **G minor** chord would be **G-Bb-D**.

A **seventh chord** is a major chord with one extra note. The extra note is the flatted seventh note of the scale. A **G7 chord** would be **G-B-D-F**.

Freaky Chords

Most of the time on the banjo you will be working with major, minor and seventh chords. If you start messing around with jazz or rock & roll you are going to see some really oddball chord names like **C Augmented**. If you are going to get into that sort of situation you might want to sit down with this little chart and start exploring these chords.

- **Major chord**: 1, 3, 5 notes in the scale.
- **Minor chord**: 1, 3b, 5 notes in the scale.
- **Major 7 chord**: 1, 3, 5, 7 notes in the scale.
- **Minor 7 chord**: 1, 3b, 5, 7b notes in the scale.
- **Dominant 7 chord**: 1, 3, 5, 7b notes in the scale.
- **Diminished chord**: 1, 3b, 5b, 6 notes in the scale.
- **Augmented chord**: 1, 3, 5# notes in the scale.
- **6th chord**: 1, 3, 5, 6 notes in the scale.
- **Suspended chord**: 1, 4, 5 notes in the scale.

There are other chords. After a while you will find that they follow a set of rules. Basically, any numbers following the letter indicate additional notes other than the standard ones. The letters "**maj**" (for "major") in front of a number indicates that the 7 is *not* flatted for this chord.

Suspended chords use a 4 in place of the 3.
Diminished chords use a flatted 3 and flatted 5.
Augmented chords use a sharped 5.

Like I said before, you don't have to know this stuff to play the banjo. And to be honest I have only had to figure out a handful of chords like this in over twenty years of playing. So I don't recommend going crazy with this but it is good to know enough to understand what a guitar player means when he or she tells you that a song has an **augmented** or **suspended** chord.

Scale Weaves

Weaving a scale is a trick that I picked up hanging around with flatpick guitar players. It is a fairly easy way to "fill in" a solo but it *sounds* like you are doing something super complex.

To **weave** a scale on the banjo you are simply going to run a major scale and change the order of the notes

For this example let's use a **G** scale

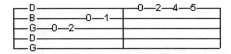

That's easy enough. Now to **weave** the scale, all we do is play three notes of the scale and then repeat the first note that we played.

```
D----------------------------------------------0-------------0-2---------
B------------0-----------0-1------0-1------0----1---------1---
G--0-2---------0-------2--------2-------
D----------------------------------------------
G----------------------------------------------
```

As you can see in this example, the first measure of the scale gets stretched out *four* measures long when you play a **weave**.

The last step in creating a scale **weave** is to break everything down into eighth notes. The easiest way to do that is by using a double thumb. I'll give you the first two measures. Try to work out the whole scale on your own.

```
D---------------------------------------------------------------
B--------------0----------0----------0---1----------2-----
G--0----2----------0----2--------------------2-----
D---------------------------------------------------------------
G-----0----0----0----0--------0----0----0-----
```

As you experiment with this technique see if you can find places to fit a measure or two into the songs you are playing. In these examples, you are only **weaving** while ascending (going up) the scale. Try the same idea while *descending* (going down) the scale. As you experiment with this technique, see if you can find places to fit a measure or two into songs you are playing.

The Blues Scale

The **blues scale** is a variation on the major scales that blues musicians use to create their distinctive solos.

I know that sounds like a canned answer, but the **blues scale** is a neat tool that can create some pretty outlandish sounds on the banjo. How it came to be and who thought it up is anyone's guess. You hear this technique a lot in electric guitar and once in a while on the banjo. You might notice a connection between the **blues scale** and **G** modal tuning.

The standard blues scale is the **1- b3 - 4 – #4 - 5 – b7 - 8** of a **major scale**. So to turn the **G major** scale into a **blues scale** you would write out your **G major scale**:

G A B C D E F# G
1 2 3 4 5 6 7 8

Pull the **1-3-4-5-7-8** notes out of the scale:

G B C D F# G

Now we flat the third by lowering it a half step, sharp the fourth by raising it a half step and flat the seven by lowering it a half step. Put everything into the order of the blues scale and we wind up with:

G Bb C C# D F G

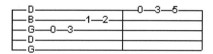

Now the big question here is "what do you do with this?"

Well that's up to you. You can use it to cook up bluesy-sounding licks like this one:

Or you could use it to swipe licks from blues guitar players like Albert King or Buddy Guy and start exploring the idea of "blues banjo." It's all up to you. Give this a shot in different spots on the fretboard using other keys and see what you get.

Pentatonic Scales

You will hear guitar players talk about **pentatonic** scales now and then. Like the **blues scale,** a **pentatonic** scale is a variation of a standard **major** or **natural minor** scale. In this case you only play five notes out of the scale.

To play a **pentatonic** scale out of a major scale, play the 1st, 2nd, 3rd, 5th, 6th, & 8th notes out of the scale. This, like the other scale patterns we have discussed, will work anywhere on the fretboard.

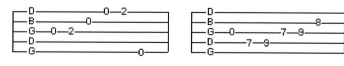

*G **major** pentatonic*   *G **major** pentatonic*

To play a **pentatonic** scale out of a **natural minor** scale, play the 1st, 3rd, 4th, 5th, 7th & 8th notes of a **natural minor** scale.

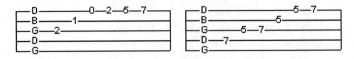

A minor pentatonic   **A minor** pentatonic

Pentatonic scales are cool because they are so easy to reach. Take a look at the second version of the each example. Both of these scales can be played while holding a chord effortlessly.

Minor chord walk-downs & passing chords

In some situations you can use the two **minor** chords out of the number system to create a **"walk down"** effect in a chord progression.

Try running a **C** chord for a few measures then switch to **Em** for half a measure and roll into an **Am.**

What is happening here is that you are using a minor version of your "**3**" chord from the number system for half a measure to lead into your relative minor chord.

When you play that **3** or **Em** chord in this fashion it is often referred to as a *passing chord*.

A **passing chord** is a chord that is played for a short period of time as a lead into a chord progression. You often see seventh chords used this way. The nice thing about a passing chord is that you don't *have* to play it. It is there for a reason but if you miss it just keep rolling with the music and try to hit it the next time around.

Try that **C** to **Am** progression again and then play it backwards. **Am** to **Em** to **C.**

Try the same thing in **G**: <u>**G** to **Bm** to **Em.**</u>

And then Try it in **D**: <u>**D** to **F#m** to **Bm.**</u>

This is a great sound effect that will really add spice to some songs.

Beyond the number system:
chord progressions within the scale

The Nashville Number System is great for figuring out chords on the fly but if you want to work out a chord progression in a minor key it gets a little clumsy.

When we talked about the **Nashville Number System** earlier in the book we numbered each note of the scale with an Arabic numeral. In a more formal music theory setting we have to use Roman numerals to number each note. This allows us to use upper case numerals for major chords and lower case numerals for minor chords.

For a **major** scale the first, fourth, fifth and eighth notes of the scale will be major chords marked with upper case numerals. The second, third and sixth notes of the scale will be minor chords marked with lower case numerals. The seventh note is ignored for now.

A C major scale marked out this way will look like this:

I   ii   iii   IV   V   vi   I

C   D   E   F   G   A   B   C

This winds up exactly the way it did for the Nashville Number System. It changes when you lay out a chord progression from a minor scale.

In a **minor** scale the first, fourth and eighth notes are marked with lower case numerals to indicate **minor chords**. The third, sixth and seventh notes are marked with upper case numbers to indicate major chords. The fifth note will be marked as a minor chord with a lower case number in a natural minor scale. In a **harmonic minor** scale the fifth note can, in some cases, wind up being played as a **major** chord. The second note in a **minor** scale, like the seventh note in a **major** scale, is ignored.

An **A minor** scale marked out this way will look like this:

i   III   iv   v   VI   VII   i

A   B   C   D   E   F   G   A

V

if the scale is a
harmonic minor

What this tells us is that in a chord progression in the key of **A minor** we can play **Am**, **C**, **Dm**, **Em** or **E**, **F** and **G**.

Laying out chord progressions this way will really help when you start to experiment with modes.

Modes

In the last chapter I brought up the interesting fact that your major scale and your natural minor scale are also **modes: Ionian (major)** and **Aeolian (natural minor.)**

Modes are a tricky subject because they are talked about quite a bit in old time music but most people really don't understand them. I've run into more than one fiddle player who got a kick out of confusing beginners at a jam by saying that a song was in **C Aeolian mode** rather than just saying the song was in **A minor.**

As I said earlier in the book, **modes** came about in the dark ages. For some reason they were given Greek names making things even more confusing because the **modes** we use today are completely different from what the ancient Greeks were working on.

Ionian mode starts the scale on the **root**, or first note of the scale. **Aeolian mode** starts on the sixth note of the scale. The other **modes** you will run into fall in between these two.

I should warn you ahead of time that we are only covering seven **modes**. There are quite a few more but the odds of running into them in a folk music context are pretty slim. If modes or any other aspect of music theory intrigues you, pick up some books on the subject or take some music theory classes at your local community college.

Let's take a look at seven **modes** in the key of **C major**:

1 2 3 4 5 6 7 8

Ionian/ Major: C D E F G A B C

Dorian: D E F G A B C D

Phrygian: E F G A B C D E

Lydian: F G A B C D E F

Mixolydian: G A B C D E F G

Aeolian/ Minor: A B C D E F G A

Locrian: B C D E F G A B

Ionian mode starts with the first note of the scale giving us a standard **C major** scale running from **C** to **C**. **Dorian mode** starts with the *second* note of the scale giving us a scale with no sharps or flats that runs from **D** to **D**.
Phrygian mode starts on the *third* note of the scale and so on.

There are two ways to look at **modes**. In one respect we are playing in **modes** all of the time on the banjo because with only four available strings, we usually wind up using part of a scale.

Sometimes a song will be in a major key but use a **modal** chord progression. For example, "**Little Maggie**" goes back and forth from the **G** to **F** chords. The song is still in **G** major but the chord progression gives it a **modal** feel.

In some cases a melody line is written specifically in a **mode**. If somebody tells you a song is in **C Dorian**, you are playing the melody from a scale starting on the second note of the **C** scale (**D**.) It's not really **C** and it's not really **Am** so it can be a little bit confusing.

It gets even crazier when you try to play rhythm for a tune played in a **mode**. In a **major** key we can use the **Nashville Number System** to play the **1-4-5** chords. In a **mode** things start to change because the whole layout and sound of the scale has changed.

It gets so confusing that some people believe that modal tunes were never *meant* to have any accompaniment. That sounds like it might be a reasonable idea until you listen around and find out that rock songs like "**The White Room**" or "**Sweet Home Alabama**" were written in modes.

Let's say the song you want to back up is in **C Dorian** mode. That means you are playing the notes of the **C major** scale from **D** to **D**. When we laid out chord progressions using Roman numerals to mark what chords would be played major or minor in a **C** scale we marked the **D** or "**2**" note as being a minor chord.

Here it is again:

I   ii iii IV V vi   I
C   D   E F G A B   C

Uppercase numerals indicate a major chord and lower case numerals indicate a minor chord.

So if **C Dorian** is starting on the **D** note we know right away that we stand a good chance that a **Dm** chord is going to fall into place somewhere in the tune. Once you know that you can try other chords used in **Dm** and figure out what will or won't work for the song. Keep in mind that you are not playing the key of **Dm** but this trick will at least give you a head start in figuring out the chord progression by ear. It's not an exact science but if you give yourself time to develop your musical ear it all starts to make sense.

Walking the scale

Another cool trick you can use is playing each chord from the scale one after the other. A run that goes **Am**, **Bm**, **C**, **D** and back to **G** makes a great ending for a tune played in the key of **G**. You can do the same thing with other keys. In order to make a run like this really stand out you want to move the progression up the neck while you are playing. For example:

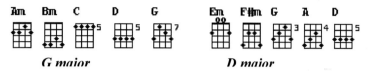

G major   *D major*

Other Time Signatures

We have played a lot of songs in 4/4 and 3/4 time up to this point but there are other time signatures that you will run into.

I know, right now you are thinking "time signatures?"

When I say that a song is in 4/4 time that four slash four or four over four is a time signature. Up to now we have just taken for granted that 4/4 means four beats to a measure and 3/4 time was three beats to a measure.

As you start to explore different kinds of music you are going to occasionally run into songs that are played in different time signatures. So it might be useful to understand just what that 4/4 symbol really means.

The number on top of a time signature tells you how many beats to play in a measure. In 4/4 time we play **four** beats to a measure and in 3/4 time it is **three** beats to a measure.

The bottom number tells you what note to count. The two time signatures that we are already familiar with (3/4 & 4/4) both tell you that the quarter note gets the beat. However the bottom number does not *always* have to be 4. It can be 1, 2, 4, 8, 16, etc.

/1 - tells you that the **whole note** gets the beat
/2 - tells you that the **half note** gets the beat
/4 - tells you that the **quarter note** gets the beat
/8 - tells you that the **eighth note** gets the beat
/16 - tells you that the **sixteenth note** gets the beat

For example:

3/4 is 3 quarter notes per measure.
5/2 is 5 half notes per measure.
6/8 is 6 eighth notes per measure.

2/4 time is used often in marches and polkas. You may also find it in old time and bluegrass music. It's almost identical to 4/4 time except that in 2/4 time you play *two* quarter notes to a measure.

"Cut time" is a variation of 4/4 time. It is actually 2/2 time. The reason that it is called "cut time" is that the note values are cut in half. For example, a half note winds up with the time value of a quarter note and a whole note winds up with the time value of a half note.

Instead of a numeric symbol cut time is marked on the staff with this symbol after the G clef.

For rhythm playing in cut time or 2/4 time I usually use the chop. Other than that it is pretty much the same as playing in 4/4 time.

6/8 time is a little bit tricky at first because it is so different from 2/4, 4/4, and 3/4 time. Your /4 time signatures are "duplet" time signatures. That just means that every beat is made up of two eighth notes (two eighth notes= one quarter note.) Your normal count in 4/4 time is:

count: 1 2 3 4   1 2 3 4   1 2 3 4   1 2 3 4

Or, if we break the measures down into eighth notes:

count: 1& 2& 3& 4&   1& 2& 3& 4&

6/8 time is a compound or "triplet" time. That means there are three eighth notes to each beat. That means the count is 1-2-3, 2-2-3 for each measure:

1 2 3 2 2 3   1 2 3 2 2 3   1 2 3 2 2 3

So in 6/8 time we have two groups of three eighth notes per measure rather than the four pairs of two eighth notes that we are accustomed to in 4/4 time.

At first this can all be pretty confusing. 6/8 time feels pretty alien the first time you work with it because we are so used to counting one, two, three, four. Your best bet is to take it slow and spend some time listening to music in 6/8 time.

Keep in mind that there are a lot of other time signatures. You might run into something as odd as 13/8 time. Therefore rather than just working out a specific picking pattern allow time to explore the nature of rhythm. It will make you a much more versatile musician and it might just open up some ideas that no one has thought of for old time banjo playing.

In some 6/8 songs like "**Oh Dear! What Can The Matter Be**?" we can play 6/8 time the same as 3/4 time. Try "**Oh Dear! What Can The Matter Be**?" in 6/8 time. Just play **bump ditty-ditty, bump ditty-ditty** for each measure. It's kind of like you are playing in double 3/4 time.

"Oh Dear! What Can The Matter Be?
6/8 Time Key of C

C

Oh Dear! | What can the matter be?

bump ditty-ditty bump ditty-ditty   bump ditty-ditty bump ditty-ditty

G7

 Oh Dear! | What can the matter be?

bump ditty-ditty bump ditty-ditty   bump ditty-ditty bump ditty-ditty

C

Oh Dear! | What can the matter be?

bump ditty-ditty bump ditty-ditty   bump ditty-ditty bump ditty-ditty

Dm   **G7**   **C**

Johnny's so   long at the | fair

bump ditty-ditty bump ditty-ditty   bump ditty-ditty bump ditty-ditty

Now if you go back and compare this to "**Who's Gonna Shoe Your Pretty little Foot**" you will notice that while the **bump ditty-ditty** is the same the phrasing of the lyrics is different. That's because rather than the 1-2-3 count that we use for 3/4 time 6/8 time is 1-2-3, 2-2-3. It has a totally different *feel* than 3/4 time.

This technique works well for singing but in an instrumental it gets a little bit more complicated.

In order to play melodies in 6/8 time we need to learn a new note symbol, the sixteenth note.

A sixteenth note ♪ has one half the value of an eighth note.

In order to play the six eighth notes to a measure for melodies in 6/8 time we sometimes have to create a picking pattern that is one eighth note followed by two sixteenth notes.

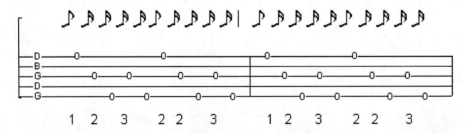

The first eighth note of the measure gets the one count while each pair of sixteenth notes gets a count of one. The count for each measure is 1-2-3 2-2-3. This will take a little bit of practice to get it smooth but don't sweat it. It is not all that different from what we were doing with double thumbing.

This pattern is not the only way to play a song in 6/8 time. Look at how we use the **hammer-on** and other techniques to change the picking pattern in 4/4 and 3/4 time. You will have to explore 6/8 time on your own and find the best way to play the music that you want to play. Let's close out this chapter with "**The Irish Washerwoman**" in 6/8 time.

"The Irish Washerwoman" A Part
6/8 Time key of G

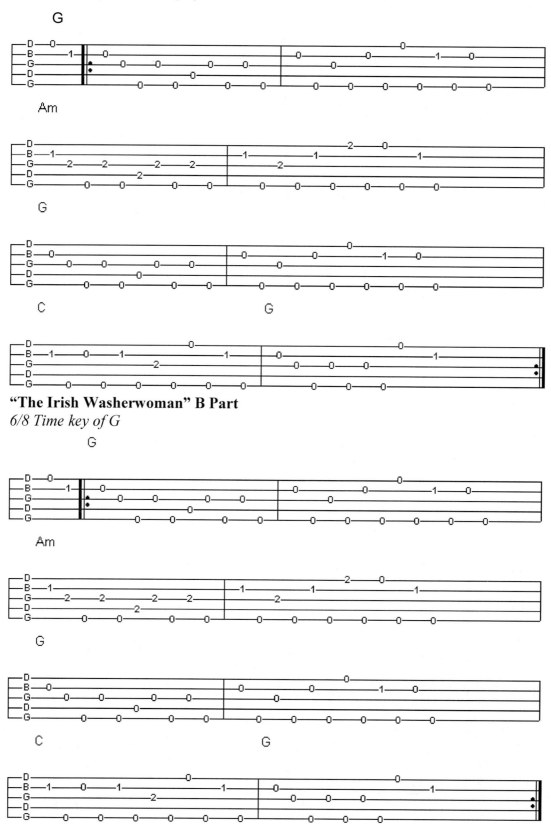

"The Irish Washerwoman" B Part
6/8 Time key of G

Alternate Tunings

To be honest 99.9% of everything I play on the banjo is in standard **open G** tuning. It has been a long time since I have even used a capo. After all these years of playing I *know* **open G** as well as I know the houses on the street where I live. But **open G** is not the only tuning available on the five-string banjo. Some people like the idea of using an exotic tuning to get them out of a rut. We are going to take a close look at two alternate tunings in this chapter just to give you an idea of what is possible.

The first tuning we are going to look at is **G modal**. To play in **G modal** tuning you simply tune the second string up to **C**. The other four strings on your banjo stay the same.

Because you have changed the tuning you will need to familiarize yourself with some new chord forms.

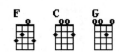

"Omie Wise"
4/4 Time Key of C G Modal Tuning: gDGCD

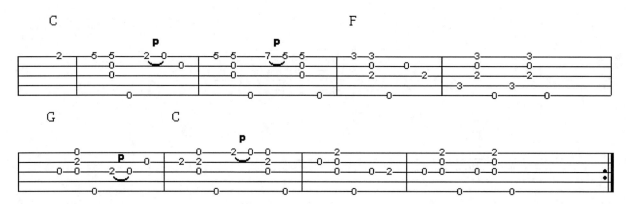

Oh listen to my story about little Omie Wise
And how she was murdered by John Lewis' lies.

He promised to meet her at Admases' Springs
He promised her money and other fine things.

She got up behind him and away they did go
Down to the River where fast waters flow.

"John Lewis, John Lewis please tell me your mind
Do you mean to marry me or leave me behind?"

"Little Omie, little Omie I'll tell you my mind,
My mind is to drown you and leave you behind."

Two little boys went fishing just at the break of dawn
They saw little Omie come floating along.

They arrested John Lewis, they arrested him today,
And they buried little Omie down in the cold clay.

This isn't exactly a happy-go-lucky song but American folk music is full of songs like this. There really *was* a Naomi Wise and a guy named John Lewis really *did* murder her. Other true-crime songs include Tom Dooley, Pretty Polly, Down In The Willowy Garden, Banks of the Ohio and countless others. You don't have to use **G Modal** tuning for this song. It will work just as well in a **minor** key out of **G** tuning:

Am   **G**
Oh listen to my story about little Omie Wise
   Am   **Em**   **Am**
and how she was murdered by John Lewis' lies.

You don't *have* to retune to play in
G modal. Take a look at the **C** and **F** chord diagrams for
this tuning again. Then compare them to the same chords
in **G** tuning.

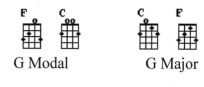

G Modal   G Major

You might notice that the only difference is the second string. So if you fret the second string at
the first fret you can use your "free" fingers to get the **G modal** sound and feeling without
retuning.

Let's try a **G modal** song out of **open G** tuning.

"**Cluck Old Hen**" is a really odd sounding old tune, but it is kind of cool in a freaky sort of way.
To make this **G modal** tune work in **open G** tuning you are going to have to keep your index
finger on the second string at the first fret throughout the tune. This will feel a little awkward at
first but if you stay with it for a while you will see that almost all of your notes and chords are
still within easy reach.

You will run into an unusual lick at the last measures of the A & B parts of "**Cluck Old Hen**." It
is variation of the **drop-thumb**.

In this lick you strike the first string with your fingernail and
swing your thumb down to hit the second string but while you
are thumbing the second string you are also playing a
phantom hammer-on on the third string at the third fret.

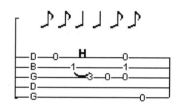

As you might notice in the rhythm line over the tab, the
hammer-on is given a quarter note time value.

"**Cluck Old Hen**"
4/4 time **G** Tuning- played as **G modal**

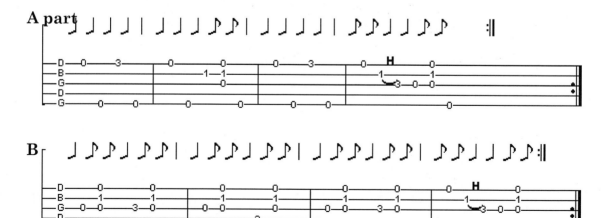

Another easy to use alternate tuning is **G minor** tuning. When we played in **G modal** we tuned
the second string up to **C**. In **G minor** tuning we tune the second string **down** to **B♭**. This tunes
your banjo to a **G minor** chord.

And like we did with **G modal** you will need to learn some new chords for the new tuning.

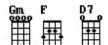

"Days of 49"
4/4 Time Key of Gm

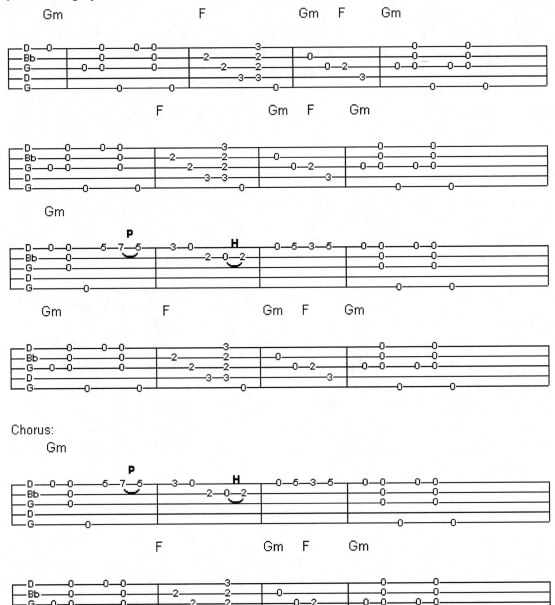

Oh here you see old Tom Moore a relic of former days
and a bummer too, they call me now- but what do I care for praise?
For my heart is filled with the days of yore, and oft do I repine
for the days of old, the days of gold, the days of '49.

I'd comrades who loved me well, a jovial saucy crew
they were some hard cases I must confess
but still they were brave and true.
Who'd never flinch whatever the pinch, would never fret or whine
like good old bricks they stood the kicks in the days of '49.

118

There was New York Jake, a butcher boy he was always getting tight.
And every time that he got full he was always hunting a fight.
One night he run up against a knife in the hands of old Bob Kline
And over Jake they held a wake in the days of '49.

There was poor old Jess, the old lame cuss He never would relent.
He never was known to miss a drink or ever spend a cent.
At length old Jess like all the rest who never would decline,
In all his bloom went up the flume in the days of '49.

There was roaring Bill from Buffalo I never will forget.
He would roar all day and he'd roar all night and I guess he's roaring yet.
One night he fell in a prospector's hole in a roaring bad design,
in that hole roared out his soul in the days of '49

Of all the comrades I had then not one remains to toast
they have left me in my misery like some poor wandering ghost.
And as I go from place to place folks call me a traveling sign.
Saying "Here's Tom Moore, A bummer sure, from the days of '49."

If you think this is a pretty long old tune I should tell you that this is not even half of the lyrics for **"Days of '49."** I had a friend who could literally sing verses for this song all night long.

Just like **G modal** you can play in **G minor** while keeping your banjo in **open G** tuning. Just use your **Gm** and **F** chords. Give it a shot on **"Days of '49."**
When you work on the songs in this chapter keep in mind that while alternate tuning changes the way you make chords it doesn't change anything with the picking hand. Each of these songs follows the **bump dit-ty** strum pretty closely.

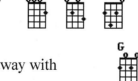

G tuning

Another very popular alternate tuning is **double C** tuning. While **G modal** and **G minor** tunings give you a sort of unusual atmosphere **double C** came about as a way to make songs in the key of **C** easier to play on the banjo. The only problem with that idea is that the key of **C** is already pretty easy to play in **open G** tuning. You have been playing in **C** since early on in this book!

That said, some players do find **double C** tuning useful for select songs. It is up to you to decide when and where to use it.

In **double C** tuning you are going to tune your forth and second strings to **C** Giving you these new chord positions to work with.

You might notice that making an *actual* **G** chord is kind of awkward. 99% of the time you can get away with making your G chord like this:

"Way Down The Old Plank Road" is a great old song that Uncle Dave Macon used to play at the Grand Ole Opry.

"Way Down The Old Plank Road"
4/4 Time Key of C

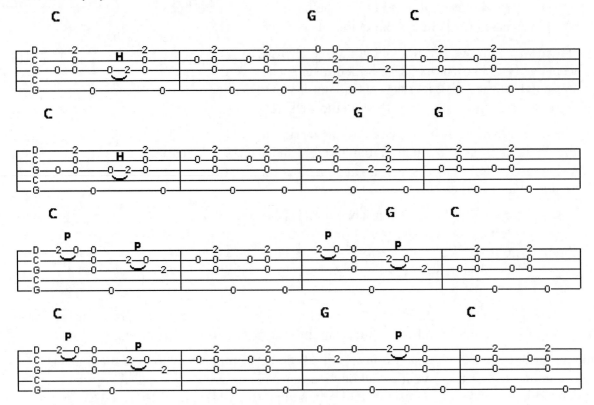

Rather be in Richmond, midst all the hail and rain,
Than for to be in Georgia boys, wearing that ball and chain.

Chorus:
Won't get drunk no more, won't get drunk no more,
Won't get drunk no more, way down on the old plank road.

I went down to Mobile for to get on the gravel train,
Very next thing heard of me, had on a ball and chain.

Dony, oh dear Dony, what makes you treat me so?
Caused me to wear the bail and chain, now my ankle's sore.

There are an almost endless number of alternate tunings for the 5-string banjo. The tunings covered here only scratch the surface.

There is **D** tuning where you tune your banjo strings **f#DFAD**.

F tuning where your strings are tuned **aDGCD**.

Single C tuning where you tune the fourth string down to **C**.

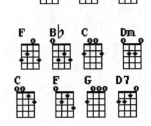

There are countless others. You don't *have* to use them but then again there is no reason *not* to use them. Decide for yourself.

120

Other Picking Patterns

The frailing strum that we have been working with up to this point is an amazingly adaptable picking style but like anything else it does have it's limits. From time to time you will run into a song in a rhythm or a key that just will not work with frailing.

Rather than box yourself in and say, "I can't play *that* kind of music" it might be helpful to have a few other arrows in your quiver. The basics of rhythm that you learned with frailing can be applied in other ways that will open up a lot more music for you to play on your banjo.

Strumming

The first alternate picking pattern we will look at is **strumming**.

The idea is simple enough. You could start out with something really basic like just strumming down the strings of your banjo with your fingers giving each strum a quarter note value (in other words, four strums to a measure.) You could go back to the mini-songbook earlier in the book and work up some tunes that way.

But if you are backing up your voice or just want to add some interesting stuff to a tune you could break up that four quarter note rhythm to come up with a more "bluesy" or Dixieland sounding type of strum.

You could start off by **chopping** and/or **vamping** while you strum or you could change the rhythm of your strum. Rather than have me tell you exactly what to do I think it would be better in the long run if you thought this one out on your own. Kick back and ask yourself *how* you could **strum** a rhythm.

You have a few options when it comes to **strumming** rhythm:

- You can strum up
- You can strum down
- You can alternate between strumming up and down
- You can pick a single note
- You can strum two, three or four strings at the same time
- You can strum with a flatpick
- You can strum with your fingers or just your thumb

I would suggest that you start exploring music that isn't really associated with old time banjo. Look around (or "listen around") and start exploring other rhythms. The shuffle rhythm of blues or the rhythm patterns in Reggae music might catch your ear. Maybe you want to try out some Dixieland material. Go crazy with this stuff but at the same time keep practicing your basic frailing skills.

One tricky part of **strumming** is the fifth string. In some keys like **F** or **Bb** the fifth string isn't going to sound right. You can retune or capo the fifth string to match the key you are playing in. You can fret the fifth string. You can also do what I do which is to just let my thumb ride the fifth when I am **strumming**. This mutes the string so that it is out of the way and it also gives me a bit of an anchor for my **strum**. Try a few different things and use whatever works best for you.

One of my favorite songs to strum on the banjo is "**St. James Infirmary Blues**." This is an old, old song that is a lot of fun to play even if it's subject matter is a little bit dark.

"St. James Infirmary Blues"

4/4 Time Key of **Dm**

```
Dm              A       Dm
```
It was down in old Joe's barroom

```
Dm          Gm     Dm
```
on the corner by the square

```
Dm              A         Dm
```
the drinks they were served as usual

```
Dm           A        Dm
```
and the usual crowd was there

On my left stood Big Joe McKennedy
His eyes were bloodshot red
He turned 'round to face the barroom
And these are the very words he said

I went down to the St. James Infirmary
I saw my sweetheart there
Lying on the table so cold, so white, so fair

I went down to see the doctor
"She's very low" he said
I went back to see my baby
And great God she was dead

And that is the end of my story
Bartender pour another round of booze
And if anyone should happen to ask you
I've got the St. James Infirmary blues.

Sometimes you will find yourself in a situation where you have to play rhythm from a lead sheet. The trick to that isn't so much paying attention to the notes as much as the note values.

I dug around in a box of old lead sheets leftover from my time playing in a Philadelphia Mummers string band and found an old gem of a tune called "**A Shanty In Old Shantytown**." This was one of the first tunes I ever worked out from a lead sheet and after all these years it still makes me smile. It's not an easy tune but it's not impossible. It's in the key of **F** so you probably won't be using the fifth string. Let's take a look at it and see what we can come up with.

A Shanty In Old Shanty Town

F   A   D7

It's only a shanty in old shanty town the

G7   F#9   G9 G7   G

roof is so slanty it touches the ground but my

C7 Bdim C7   F   Bb Bbm F   D7

tumbled down shack by the old railroad track like a

G7   G9 Bbdim G7   C9   C7

millionaire's mansion is calling me back I'd

F   A   D7   G7

give up a palace if I were a king it's more than a

F#9   G9   G   G   Bb   Edim Bb   Bbm

palace it's my everything there's a queen waiting there with a

F A7 D7   Gm   Bdim C7

silvery crown in a shanty in old shanty

F   F Bbm

town.

I can almost hear you saying "**E dim**? **F#9**? Is he out of his *mind*?"

Don't sweat the freaky chords. This is where we use a musical term called **chord substitution** which is a fancy way of saying "Leave out the chords you don't know how to play" or, to put it more bluntly, "fudging it."

The **F#9** chord sounds *almost* exactly like an **F#7** chord. So you can use an **F#7** chord instead of an **F#9**. If you don't know how to make an **F#7** chord you can get away with an **F#** chord but we're starting to push it just a little bit. If you can't make an **F#7** chord you shouldn't be reading this part of the book yet.

The **E dim** and **G9** chords are *passing* chords. A passing chord has such a short duration (one or two beats) that nobody will ever notice if you don't play it.

So the first step to tackling a lead sheet is to substitute the chords you can't play and then chuck out the chords that you don't need.

Wade through the passing chords. See what you can take away and streamline without losing the overall *feel* of the song.

Don't think of this as cheating. I've been playing this song for a long, long time and I still ditch a passing chord or two when I play it.

Let's clean up this lead sheet and see if it makes any more sense.

It's   only   a   shanty   in   old shanty town   the

roof is so   slanty   it   touches   the   ground   but my

tumbled down   shack   by the   old   railroad   track   like   a

millionaire's   mansion   is   calling me back   I'd

give up a   palace if   I were a king   it's more than   a

palace it's   my everything   there's a   queen waiting   there with a

silvery   crown   in a   shanty in   old shanty

town.

Now it's a little bit more doable.

The next step is to strum the rhythm. The melody is written out in standard notation but as a rhythm player what you want to look at is the note values of each measure.

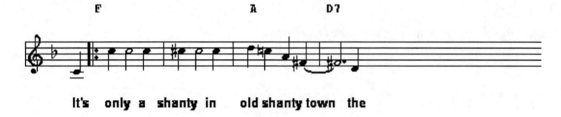

The first few measures <u>are all quarter and half notes</u>. You can play a simple down-stroke rhythm of four strums a measure. Or you could play up and down. Or you could chop the rhythm.

In the long run it's up to you. Explore some strumming patterns and see what you can come up with. And have fun with "**A Shanty In Old Shanty Town**." I have had some great times playing this song.

Bluegrass & Fingerstyle Banjo

It's thought of today as bluegrass or "Scruggs style" banjo but what we now call bluegrass banjo is just a finger picking variation of the frailing strum. It's hard to say exactly which came first, up picking or down picking. In the end none of that is really important. The neat thing is that if you have your basic right and left hand techniques under a reasonable amount of control you can add some finger picking or bluegrass banjo skills to your bag of tricks.

In bluegrass banjo the **bump dit-ty** is replaced with a string of eighth notes. The picking pattern for this string of eighth notes is usually referred to as a roll.

The best way to understand what a roll "is" would be to try a few out.

Set your picking hand with your ring or pinky finger (or both) resting on the head of your banjo and with either three fingers (your thumb, index and middle) or two fingers (thumb and index) try picking some of these eighth note rolls. Keep in mind that when we are counting eighth notes we count 1 & 2 & 3 & 4 &.

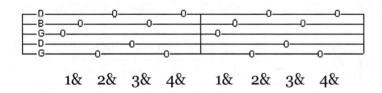

Now the other thing to think about here is the right hand technique involved with picking a roll like this.

One of the odd things that happened with bluegrass style banjo is that people seemed to stop looking at the instrument or the style objectively. A lot of players will obsess about the exact hand position that a well-known banjo picker uses and try to copy it.

My advice is to compare this technique to what you already know and find an approach that works for you. Keep in mind that this is a lot like frailing in that nothing matters but the rhythm. As long as you can keep that eighth note picking pattern smooth you are good to go.

If you start getting serious about exploring this approach to the banjo you will begin to develop a right hand technique on your own. Odds are that you won't even realize you are doing it.

Here are a few more rolls to experiment with. Once you can play these you can start working on keeping the picking pattern smooth while changing chords.

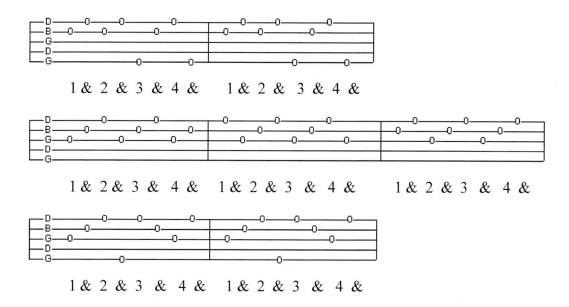

1 & 2 & 3 & 4 &   1 & 2 & 3 & 4 &

1 & 2 & 3 & 4 &   1 & 2 & 3 & 4 &   1 & 2 & 3 & 4 &

1 & 2 & 3 & 4 &   1 & 2 & 3 & 4 &

Once you can play a roll smoothly add in your left hand techniques.

All the tools that you used for frailing can be dropped right into three-finger bluegrass style banjo. The only thing that has changed is the right hand picking pattern.

Give these rolls a shot with an alternate tuning. Come up with your own picking patterns. Figure out ways to add in quarter notes and sixteenth notes. Work out some blues scale licks. Figure out how to play a fingerstyle roll in keys that are not quite so fifth string friendly such as **E**. Listen to guitar players like Mississippi John Hurt or Reverend Gary Davis and see if you can adapt some of the patterns they used to the banjo.

Another approach to finger picking the banjo is to play a series of notes that do not have the "flow" of the eighth note roll found in bluegrass.

This style of banjo has been around for a long time but players like Charlie Poole and Doc Boggs popularized it in the twenties and thirties.

The trick here is to play a rhythm and pretty much ignore the melody line. You are still following a chord progression but most of the time you are not putting an emphasis on the melody notes. The end result is a little jarring the first time you hear it but in some situations it's kind of cool.

Rather than pick apart an individual players' technique I'll do the same thing I did with the bluegrass rolls and just give you some ideas to start experimenting with.

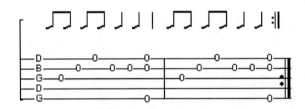

In this lick you can see that it's a fairly simple picking pattern. Once you can do this with an open **G** chord try keeping it going through some chord changes. You might also notice that this example follows a quarter note-two eighth note rhythm just like the basic frailing strum.

This example is built around a **C7** chord. I set it up to have just a little bit of that Doc Boggs bluesy flavor to it.

In this last example everything is changed around. Now you are playing two sets of eighth notes and *then* two quarter notes.

I'm keeping this a little bit open ended because by this point in the book you should already be making music. Going into fingerstyle should be a creative extension of what you have already learned rather than viewing it as a separate style. In fact, you can incorporate a lot of these ideas into your basic frailing strum by changing the rhythm of your right hand.

If you do decide to experiment with finger picking you may want to try out some finger picks. They come in a wide range of styles and sizes. I've even run into players who wear two picks on each finger (one covering the pad of the finger and one covering the fingernail) so that they could alternate between picking, strumming and frailing at whim. The resulting sound was . . . interesting. But it was cool because in each case the person doing the playing was doing what he or she wanted to do.

The thing to keep in mind is that if it's in rhythm, in tune, played on a banjo and it is what *you* want to do then it's cool. Play what you love and play what you feel.

Chord Melody

Chord melody is a complex technique used extensively by four string banjo players. The idea behind this technique is to create a chord around each note in the melody. To pull that off you need a pretty extensive background in music theory and some really top-notch instrumental skills. It would take another book to explain how tenor and plectrum banjo players make this all work together.

We don't have to get that technical here because we won't be using strummed chords to create melody lines all that often on the five-string banjo (unless you want to.) But we can use the idea now and then to spice up a song.

Everybody knows the melody to "**The Star Spangled Banner**"
(but as lieutenant Frank Drevin pointed out in *Police Squad* nobody can ever remember the words) so that's as good a tune as any to introduce some chord melody. Let's voice out the melody to the song by moving around our **G**, **C** and **D** chords.

I've laid out the first verse of the song with a chord diagram over each word. Treat "Oh" like a pickup note and starting with "say" strum a new chord as you sing each word of the song.

I'm not really worried about the rhythm of the song here. The idea is just to demonstrate how you can use chord changes to create a melody effect. I usually just give each word and chord one strum but as you get comfortable with the idea of changing these chords you can frail or fingerpick the tune.

"The Star Spangled Banner"

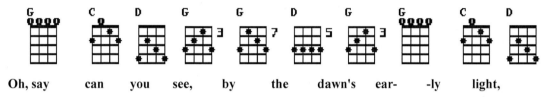

If you roll this exercise through your head for a while you might be able to come up with some really cool effects in other songs. If you add in techniques like **chopping**, **vamping**, **chord bouncing** and even **hammer-on's** or **pull-off's** you all of a sudden have a very powerful tool in your arsenal of banjo picking styles.

Try to work out the chord melody for the rest of "**The Star Spangled Banner**" on your own. I put a list of the chords I use for this song after the lyrics but don't be afraid to try some chord variations of your own.

"The Star Spangled Banner"

Oh, say can you see, by the dawn's early light,

What so proudly we hailed at the twilight's last gleaming?

Whose broad stripes and bright stars, through the perilous fight,

O'er the ramparts we watched, were so gallantly streaming?

And the rockets' red glare, the bombs bursting in air,

Gave proof through the night that our flag was still there.

O say, does that star-spangled banner yet wave,

O'er the land of the free and the home of the brave

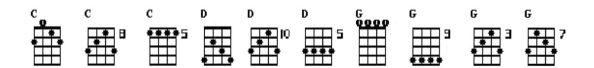

Reading Music

If you have been playing the banjo for any length of time you have probably heard somebody say, "banjo players don't read music."

It's a popular misconception that reading music is out of the grasp of the average banjo player. I'm not sure why people believe this. Then again, I know a guy who is convinced that Elvis is coming back in a flying saucer someday soon with a bunch of little green guys to teach us all how to dance the peppermint twist and make gasoline out of cheeseburgers and old sweat socks.

In other words, people get some pretty bizarre ideas now and then.

Reading music isn't hard. In fact you *already* know how to read music. You just don't know it yet. Let's go back to the chromatic scale.

Like I said earlier the notes we use in Western music are labeled
A through **G** with a half step between each note.

A | B C | D | E F | G |

Now let's write out the chromatic scale without the half steps.

A B C D E F G

To understand written music the first trick is to realize that the seven letters we just wrote out repeat over and over again in either direction.

A B C D E F G A B C D E F G A B C D E F G A B C D E F G A B

Now if these seven notes repeat over and over again you will need some kind of reference point when you read music. The old guys and gals who devised the system of standard musical notation came up with a pretty neat solution.

The funky little squiggle at the beginning of the staff is a **G clef**. The reason it's called a **G clef** is because the big spiral ends on the **G** line of the staff.

      G

Now let's go back to the layout of the chromatic scale again:

A B C D E F G

If the **G clef** marks the **G** line the space directly *below* that line has to be **F** and the space *above* that line has to be **A**.

That's all there is to it. That string of seven notes is repeated over and over again and your reference point is the **G line** marked by the **G clef.**

So if we worked our way up from the **G line**:

G   A   B   C   D   E   F

Or down from the **G line**:

G   F   E

Now you are not limited to the lines of the staff. When a note goes beyond the lines you can keep the whole deal going by adding more lines. These extra lines are called **ledger lines**.

Here's how it works:

G   A   B   C   G   F   E   D   C   B   A

Nothing to it, right?

The only tricky part to all of this is that you need to know the notes on your banjo in order to play the notes on the staff. Remember, as I said back in the chapter on scales, knowing all of the notes on your fretboard is not a big deal.

If you have your first string tuned to a **D** note (and if you are working out of **G** tuning it *is* tuned to **D**) the note at the first fret has to be the next step in the chromatic scale.

D, D#/Eb, E, F, F#/Gb, G G#/Ab, A, A#/Bb, B, C, C#/Db and so on.

So the first string open is a **D** note. At the first fret you get a **D#** or **Eb.** At the second fret you get an **E** note and so on.

For a visual example of this let's walk down the first seven frets of each string. I will give you both the tab and the written notation.

First String:

D D# E F   F# G G# A

```
--D--0--1--2--3-----4--5--6--7--
--B-----------------------------
--G-----------------------------
--D-----------------------------
--G-----------------------------
```

Second String:

B C C# D   D# E   F   F#

Third String:

G G# A A#   B   C C# D

Fourth String:

D D# E F   F# G G# A

One thing you might want to look at twice is how things change in the written notation for the first and fourth strings.

Your first thought might be "What changes? They're both tuned to **D**" and that's true except that *the fourth string is tuned lower than the first string*. Take a look at the notation for the two strings again. You will see that while both show the same notes the fourth string is marked out lower on the staff.

That should help you figure out that written music doesn't just tell us which note to play. It also gives the pitch.

Another symbol on the staff you need to be aware of is the
key signature.

Each scale, along with its relative minor scale, has a unique number of sharps or flats. For instance, in the key of **G** the **F** note is played as an **F sharp** (**F#**.) In order to avoid having to put the "**#**" symbol in front of each **F** note we just mark it once in the key signature.

For example, if we wanted to write out "**Skip To My Lou**" in the key of **G** without a key signature we would have to place a sharp symbol ("#") in front of each F note:

By using the **key signature** for the key of **G** we don't have to sharp the **F** note because the key signature tells us that each **F** note is played as **F#**:

Here are the key signatures for a few different keys.

The key of **C** has no sharps or flats so the key signature is left blank. The key of **D** has two sharps so the key signature shows two sharp signs. The key of **A** has three sharps. The key of **F** has one flat.

Keep in mind that the key signature shows the number of sharps or flats in a given key.

The next symbol on the staff is the time signature. You already know about 4/4 and 3/4 time from an earlier chapter.

Key of A in 4/4 time

Sometimes instead of a numeric time signature 4/4 will be marked with a **C** for "**common time.**"

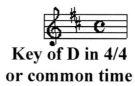

**Key of D in 4/4
or common time**

For 2/2 or "**cut time**" you might see the **C** symbol with a slash through it.

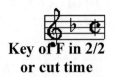

Key of F in 2/2
or cut time

You will also occasionally run into notes called **accidentals**. These are notes that are played in a way (sharp, flat or natural) different from how they are normally played in a given key.

F   F   F
Sharp flat natural

In some songs you may also run into **dotted notes**.
A dotted note has the full value of the note *plus half*.

||:Keep in mind that **repeat signs** face each other.   :||

A **double bar** marks the end of a piece of music. ||

There are other symbols you will run into. You can learn more about them as you go along.

Now let's see if we can plunk out a melody. The first song we played at the beginning of the book was "**Skip To My Lou**" so I guess that's a good tune to use for this.

"Skip To My Lou"

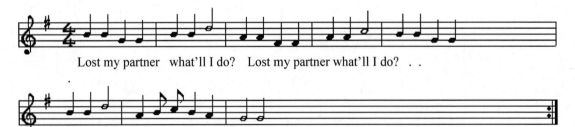

Lost my partner what'll I do?   Lost my partner what'll I do? . .

First of all, what key are we playing this in?

If you said "**G**" give yourself a pat on the back.

Now what's the time signature?
If you said 4/4 time you've got this wired!

Now if you look at the first measure you have four quarter notes: two "B" notes and two "G" notes. Look at this and run it through your head a few times. You'll see that this is really easy to play on the banjo. Your second string is tuned to *B* and your third string is tuned to *G* so you don't even have to fret a string in the first measure!

Here's the first few measures of "**Skip To My Lou**" in tab to help you get started.

Lost my partner   what'll I do?   Lost my partner what'll I do?   . . .

That's *one* way to play it but you don't *have* to play it there. The notation is written to show a particular pitch for the song but you can play the notes anywhere on the fretboard.

Here are the same four measures played up the neck:

```
 D—9—9——————9—9-12——7—7—————————7—7-10——
 B—————8—8————————————————7—7——————————
 G—————————————————————————————————————
 D—————————————————————————————————————
 G—————————————————————————————————————
```

Lost my partner   what'll I do?   Lost my partner what'll I do?   . . .

That leads us to the next step of interpreting written music.

I know what you are thinking, "what is there to interpret? It's all written down for me, right?"

Well sort of. Take another run through "**Skip To My Lou**." You can pick out the melody and call it a song but it doesn't sound all that cool. It just sounds like somebody plunking out single notes.

The trick is to take the written melody line and play it in a way that gives the song some life.

What I usually do first is figure out the chord progression. The first time that you play the melody line look at the notes and see if the fingering is on or around any chord forms. Try a few different chord forms and then use the **Nashville Number System** to get an idea of the chord progression.

This isn't an exact science. You'll have to try this over and over again until you develop a feel for how chord progressions work.

We know from playing "**Skip To My Lou**" earlier that the song goes back and forth from **G** to **D7**. Even if we didn't know this we should see that the notes in the third measure all fall into a **D** or **D7** chord position.

Once you know the chord progression it's no big deal to just play your basic **bump dit-ty** strum and change chords with the music.

Do that a few times and then go back to the sheet music and start mixing the melody line into your **bump dit-ty** strum.

This isn't as big a deal as it might sound. Take another look at the first four measures of "**Skip To My Lou**." In the first measure you have four quarter notes. If you cut two of those quarter notes in half you can drop in a **bump dit-ty** because, you guessed it, half of a quarter note is an eighth note and the **dit-ty** is made up of two eighth notes.

In the second measure you can cut the half note in half and then break one of the two resulting quarter notes in half again.

What you wind up with is the melody line of the song sort of floating over the **bump dit-ty** rhythm.

I'll tab out the first four measures of "**Skip To My Lou**" for you. Then you can work out the rest of the tune on your own.

One thing to keep in mind is that you don't have to play every note that's written down on paper. The cool thing about frailing is that the rhythm fills up the song to a point where your audience starts hearing the melody line in their heads.

I know that might sound a little crazy at first but great music is interactive. The person listening gets caught up in the rhythm and starts interacting with the song. As the old timers used to say, "if you get their feet tapping you've got 'em!"

Also keep in mind that you don't have to frail every song. Try playing something with a bluegrass roll or mixing up chord melody with some kind of picking pattern. Use your imagination. Be creative.

The way I would normally suggest approaching a song is to get a feel for the lyrics (if there are any) and an idea of the chord progression.

I'm also fully aware that you are going to dive right into the sheet music anyway so why fight it?

Here's the melody line for the first tune. It's and old, old song called "**Barbara Allen**."

"Barbara Allen"

I'm sure that you have heard this tune somewhere. It's been sung by just about everyone including Porky Pig.

Let's see what we've got here. The key signature has one sharp so what key are we going to be playing in?

If you said "**G**" you've got it.

So the song is in 3/4 time in the key of **G**.

Now try picking out the melody. The first two notes are rests. Rests are cool because you get to do just that- rest. The first measure ends with a single eighth note.

In the second measure you have two eighth notes and a dotted quarter note. Remember that a dotted note has its full value *plus half*.

In order to help you get started I'll tab out the first couple of measures for you.

```
D-----------------------------0---------------------------------0--5--5------
B--------------------0--1--------------1----0------------0-------------------
G-------------0-------------------------------2--0----2----------------------
D---------------------------------------------------------------------------
G---------------------------------------------------------------------------
```

Keep in mind that your first string at the fifth fret is the same note as your fifth string so you can use either one, or even both, in the fourth measure.

Just experiment with the notes a little bit and see if you can pick out something that sounds like a melody. Then take a look at the lyrics. See you can match the melody to the words of the song.

Now let's look at the music again *with* the lyrics.

"Barbara Allen"

In Scarlet Town where I was born	"O don't you remember in yonder town
There was a fair maid dwelling	When we were at the tavern?
Made Many a youth cry well-a-day	You gave a health to the ladies round
Her name was Barbara Allen	And you slighted Barbara Allen"
It was in the merry month of May	"O yes I remember in yonder town
when the green buds they were swelling	When we were at the tavern
Sweet William came to the West Country	I gave a health to the ladies round
And he courted Barbara Allen	Gave my heart to Barbara Allen"
He sent his servant unto her	Then lightly tripped she down the stairs
To the place where she was dwelling	She heard those church bells tolling
Said my master's sick, bids me call for you	And each bell seemed to say as it tolled
If your name be Barbara Allen	"Hard hearted Barbara Allen"
Well slowly, slowly got she up	"O mother, mother, go make my bed
And slowly she went nigh him	And make it long and narrow
But all she said as she passed his bed	Sweet William died for me today
"Young man I think you're dying"	I'll die for him tomorrow"
"O yes, I'm sick, & very sick	The buried Barbara in the old church yard
And death is in me dwelling	They buried Sweet William nigh her
Unless I have the love of one	Out of his grave grew a red, red rose
The love of Barbara Allen	And out of hers a briar
	They grew and grew up the old church wall
	Till they could grow no higher
	And at the top twined in a lovers' knot
	The red rose & the briar

Now as you pluck/plunk out the melody line sing the song and fish around for the chords.

That isn't as big of a deal as you might think.

Remember that most but not all of the songs you run into in folk music are going to follow the 1-4-5 chord progression.

This arrangement of "**Barbara Allen**" is in the key of **G**. If we remember the **Nashville Number System** we know that we can use a **G**, **C** and **D** chord progression for this song.

If we go back and look at the melody we can get an idea of the chord progression just by looking at the notes.

I'll show the first four measures in tablature again so that it is easier to visualize.

```
 D ─────────────┬──────────0──────┬───────────┬───────0──5──5─────────────
 B ─────────────┤───0───1───────1─┤───0───────┤───0───────────────────────
 G ─────────0───┤─────────────────┤─────2─0─2─┤───────────────────────────
 D ─────────────┤─────────────────┤───────────┤───────────────────────────
 G ─────────────┴─────────────────┴───────────┴───────────────────────────
```

The first two measures look like it could be a **G** chord. Then it might go into a **D** or **D7**.

Let's try it and see.

G   **D**   **G**
In Scarlet Town where I was born

That feels like it works. Now go through the rest of the song and figure out the other chords on your own.

Once you can sing the song and play a simple rhythm accompaniment you will find that blending in the melody from the sheet music is pretty easy. That's an important thing to keep in mind as you work on the next couple of songs on your own. Remember, the melody is nice but it's the rhythm that makes everything work. Get the rhythm down first and add in the melody line as you go along.

Now let's take a look at a more complicated song. I've always liked the old Irish reel "**The Silver Spear**" because it sounds a lot harder than it really is and it's got a cool name to boot.

"The Silver Spear"

Ok, the key signature has two sharps so what key are we playing in?

139

If you said **"D"** we are good to go.

Playing a song in the key of **D** will be a lot easier if we brush up on the **D** scale.

If you look at the melody line you can see that most of the A part is played right out of your **D** chord.

I'll tab out the first few measures so this is easier to see:

Now you've got the notes but the rhythm might seem a little bit freaky. Even more so when you stop to think that this time around we don't have any lyrics to help us with the phrasing of the song!

Don't sweat it. Think back to how we counted different groups of quarter notes and eighth notes.

Now take a look at the rhythm of the pick up notes and the first two measures:

I'm sure you can come up with more than one way to play that rhythm on your banjo. Try a few different techniques and see what works best for how you want to play the song.

That strange little ">" symbol over some notes is an accent mark. You want to emphasize those accented notes in order to make the melody clearer over the rhythm. Experiment with it and see what you can come up with.

The **A** part (in the first set of repeat symbols) works fine out of your **D** chord but the **B** part goes to a higher pitch. It may be easier to play the **B** part out of a different chord position. Try the **G** position **D** chord at the seventh fret.

Let's try a few more songs before we close out this chapter.

"Si Beg Si Mor" is Gaelic for something like "big hill, little hill" or "big fairy hill, little fairy hill." The only Irish my great grandmother would teach my father was the Gaelic for "go away you're a pain in the ass" so I'm not 100% sure of the exact translation.

Whatever the name means it's a beautiful song written by a blind harpist named O'Carolan who wandered around Ireland in the late sixteen hundreds and the early seventeen hundreds writing melodies as gifts to his patrons. It's hard to believe that a tune jotted down to pay a bar tab could wind up being loved by so many people for so many years.

Everybody who plays this song seems to put his or her own stamp on it. I've heard it played sad and slow and I've heard it played quick and bright. Either way it's still one of the prettiest melodies I've ever heard.

"Si Beg Si Mor"

You should be able to glance at the sheet music and know that we are playing the song in the key of **C** in **3/4** time. The melody is simple enough to plunk out but it will take a little bit of thought to figure out where to play this on the fretboard and how you want the song to come across.

"Ryan's Polka" is a tune near and dear to my heart because I used to play it with an Irish band when I was in high school. The band was from Belfast and I was sort of the fill-in musician whenever the accordion player got smashed.

I filled in a *lot*.

The guys in the band used to call this tune "Boom-Boom." Here in the states it's always referred to as **"Ryan's Polka"** but I think "Boom-Boom" is a cooler name for the tune. You can call it whatever you want to.

Work this one out on your own using what you have learned from the other tunes.

"Ryan's Polka" or "Boom-Boom"

Ok, enough with the Celtic stuff.

"Barlow Knife" is a nifty little fiddle tune with three parts. When you are working on this one you can play each part twice. When you get to a jam session ask the fiddler how many times to play each part.

I'll toss in a handful of other tunes in after **"Barlow Knife**

Have Fun!

"Barlow Knife"

"Dark Eyes"
Russian folk song

"Golden Slippers"

143

"The Girl I Left Behind Me"

My Darling Asleep

The *Tao* of old-time banjo

The word Tao means, literally, "way."

The word comes from ancient China and was used by some pretty interesting philosophers like Lao Tzu as a way of explaining that things sometimes work better when you just follow your own path.

When I sat down to put this book together I wanted to present the basic skills you would need to find your own "way" to making music on the five-string banjo. I also didn't want to put too much of my own stamp on the techniques I was sharing. The best solution I could come up with was to break the book into two parts. A "How" section that just laid out the tools and a "Tao" section that offered some friendly advice on what you could *do* with those tools.

The upcoming pages are little more than a collection of anecdotes and ideas presented with no intention other than to make you laugh and maybe give you a gentle nudge so that you will take your banjo out the front door and go have some adventures.

Going With The Flow

I was sitting on a broken guitar amp playing my banjo in this hole-in-the-wall music shop on the outskirts of town when the Irish guy walked in.

"Is that a banjo you've got there?" He asked me.

"No," I said. "It's a new kind of tuba."

"Well if you're going to get smart with me the hell with you!" He said. "But if you want to make a couple of bucks I might have a gig for you. Do you play any Irish music?"

"Oh yeah," I said, "I can play that stuff."

So he told me to show up at this bar a good number of miles up the highway. All I had to do was stand by and be ready to step in when the accordion player got drunk. According to the Irish guy that wouldn't take too long.

I said I would be there and the Irish guy left.

"Hey Pat," the guy behind the counter asked me "do you even know any Irish music?"

I thought about it for a second. "No, can't say that I do but he doesn't know that. Besides, I'm Irish so anything I play is technically Irish music. Anyway, how hard could it be?"

The guy behind the counter cracked up. "Well, you are going to find out tonight. So how are you going to get there?" He started counting off my lack of options on his fingers "You don't drive, the buses don't run that late, you can't afford a cab and it's too freaking far to walk. So what are you gonna do?"

"I don't know and I'm not sure that I care." I replied. "If I don't get there then I don't get there. Might as well try. Better than sitting here all night."

"Yeah" The guy said, "playing your *tuba*!" He cocked his head like something just occurred to him "Hey Pat, ain't you supposed to be in school?"

So I went home and got some decent clothes on. I didn't tell my folks where I was going. I didn't think my parents would have been thrilled to hear that their sixteen year old son was heading off to play all night in an Irish bar with no way to get there and no way to get home.

Getting there was going to be tricky. The guy at the music store was right on all counts but I figured if I pointed myself in the general direction of the bar and got started something would happen. I told myself that an object in motion tends to stay in motion and started walking.

I left plenty early in case I had to walk all the way there. I got to the highway and it started to rain. I broke open my banjo case and got out my banjo. A little bit of rain wouldn't hurt it and I figured somebody would notice a kid playing the banjo on the side of the highway in the rain and offer me a ride.

So I'm sitting on my case by the side of the highway playing my banjo in the rain trying to keep my cigarette from getting wet looking for all the world like an extra from the "Grapes of Wrath" right down to the Tom Joad cap cocked on my head. All of a sudden this car stops right in the middle of the highway and a big guy in a T-shirt with muscles all over his body and perfect hair gets out and starts jumping up and down yelling at me.

I reached in my pocket and wrapped my hand around the roll of nickels I kept in my jacket. Just in case this guy was some kind of a wacko.

He was blocking traffic and yelling at me to let him give me a ride. I threw my banjo back in its case and jumped into his car. As he started the car he started speed rapping, "You're a banjo player! I can't believe it! Thank you Jesus!"

As soon as he mentioned the "Big J" I reached in my pocket for that roll of nickels again. It seems that my driver had just given up being a male stripper to become a Pentecostal preacher. His father had given him a banjo when he left for bible school and this afternoon he had been praying for God to send him somebody to help him learn how to play the banjo.

Oh yeah.

I had the feeling I was in The Blues Brothers. If this guy started talking about being on a mission from God I didn't know what I was going to do.

He might have been wired a little bit loose in the upstairs but he was a genuinely nice guy. I talked to him about playing the banjo and wound up having dinner at his place and giving him a banjo lesson. It worked out great because he lived only a block away from the bar.

The preacher had a bit of a problem with my gig that night. He kept saying that this was not a good place. And he would be a lot happier if I would just let him give me a ride home.

"Don't sweat it." I told him "It isn't like anything is going to happen. And if something does happen I'll figure out what to do as I go along."

"Well," he said, "I'll be praying."

So I walked into the bar. I'm not going to tell you everything that happened but to make a long story short the bar was rough. The accordion player did get drunk and I did have to fill in for him. I fell in love with Irish music and wound up joining the band for a while. I walked home at about three in the morning with money in my pocket and my head full of music.

It was my first paid gig.

The next day I went down to the music store to blow some of my hard-earned cash on a set of guitar strings. The guy at the store asked me how it went.

"Nothing to it." I said.

There is a story about an old man who accidentally fell into the river rapids leading to a waterfall. All of the witnesses figured the old man had been killed but he came out alive and unharmed downstream at the bottom of the falls. People asked him how he managed to survive. "I just went with the flow of the water. Without thinking, I allowed myself to be shaped by it. When the water went left I went left. When the water went right I went right. After a while it started to be fun."

When some people start playing the banjo they tend to fret about controlling the situation. They always wind up getting frustrated and disappointed because you can't plan for every contingency. Sometimes you just have to go with the flow and let the river take you where it wants to go.

Like Daniel Boone once said, "If you don't care where you are you ain't lost."

Opportunities are going to pop up and disappear in a flash. If you think about it, weigh the options or waste time doubting yourself that opportunity will disappear.

Sometimes you just have to have faith. Sometimes you just have to go with the flow.

Playing well with others

When somebody comes to us for banjo lessons we always drag them, usually kicking and screaming, to a jam session as soon as they can play the basic strum and change a few chords.

You see, it's one thing to sit at home by yourself and play a few songs. It's another thing entirely to play in a group. When you are playing alone you don't know if you are screwing up the rhythm by adding an extra beat to a measure or speeding up and slowing down. In a jam session you *have* to play in rhythm with the group.

So my advice to you is to get out to a jam session as soon as you can. If you don't know about any jam sessions in your neck of the woods ask around the local music shops and maybe even put a note on the bulletin board. If that doesn't work put an ad in the local paper. If you keep your eyes open you will find some folks to pick with.

I know that right now you are reading this thinking "I'll go to a jam when I can play better." The problem with that line of thought is that if you wait until you are "good enough" you never will be. This is a *huge* part of the learning process.

Don't be self-conscious about playing in front of other musicians. Any player with a little bit of experience has been right where you are now. Somebody might crack a joke if you really screw something up big-time but overall "real" musicians are pretty patient with beginners as long as they see some progress from jam to jam. If you go to your first jam session and everybody shows you a lick and encourages you they will expect progress the next time they see you. I don't mean coming back in a month playing Bach on your banjo. The progress I'm referring to is never that dramatic.

Just go home and put some time into really working on anything the guys or gals at the jam shared with you. That way when they see you again they'll know you are not wasting their time. Nobody likes to have his or her picking time eaten up paying attention to somebody who won't practice.

Now when you go to your first jam session you are going to feel like you are the clumsiest, slowest, most out of tune and out of tempo bozo that ever picked up a banjo. As that's going through your head you're going to be thinking over and over again "but I could PLAY when I was home alone!"

Once again, everybody goes through this. You see, this is a totally new environment to you. Your brain is so busy trying to take in the new surroundings that you go into a sort of overload. I mean, you are sitting in a room full of musicians and everybody is playing and singing and you are nervous about playing in front of a bunch of strangers. You feel like there is this big blinking neon sign over your head that reads "Can't Pick A Lick."

If you keep going to the jam you will acclimate to this new environment. After you make a few mistakes and realize that nobody is going to make fun of you or slap you around you'll start to relax. Once you start to relax you'll be able to play without fighting yourself and from that point, well things just sort of start moving.

So get out and jam. Don't worry about playing perfectly because nobody ever does. Remember, folk music isn't about technical perfection. It's about fellowship.

Don't worry about playing the melody. Melody is nice but it's nothing without the rhythm holding it together. Play everything as simply as you can. Over time you'll get comfortable playing with others and you'll find that the melody sort of comes into your playing on it's own.

Cool old dudes

"What the *hell* do you think you're doing? You don't think that's the blues? My God boy, give me that guitar before you hurt somebody!"

The next thing I knew the guitar was out of my hands and the guy was touching up the tuning with one hand and lighting one of my cigarettes with the other. Cussing me the whole time.

"A nice guitar like this being played by a chump like you out in public. What's this city coming to? Marlboros? Why can't you smoke the right brand? Smart mouth little . . ."

It was all happening too fast. I was minding my business riding the subway from the 69th street terminal into the city stopping at every other station to play my guitar and make a few bucks. I'd find a corner on the platform, pick a spot to play and keep my case open in front of me. People walking by usually threw something in. Sometimes it was a used Kleenex and sometimes it was money.

Getting paid to play was kind of cool and it beat being in school as long as the police didn't roust me.

Now I had this crazy old guy swiping my cigarettes, handling my guitar and swearing at me a mile a minute. Once the shock wore off I started to get mad.

"Hey, who are you?" I said " And give me back my guitar!"

"I ain't gonna hurt your guitar, boy. And it's not like a nice white boy from the suburbs couldn't afford a new guitar. If you shut up you might learn something. I'm gonna show you something now, son. Think of it as a public service because I can't let you keep going like that. Hurt people's ears playing like that!"

Before I could say anything in my defense (I mean I wasn't *that* bad, at least I didn't think I was) the guy started playing.

Playing isn't a strong enough word. He took that guitar and just tore into it. It cried. It screamed. People on the subway platform stopped in their tracks.

The sound of my big Dobro 33H metal body guitar filled up the subway tunnel like a wind. Stuffy looking guys in business suits started bobbing their heads and tapping their feet. A couple of people started clapping along and a scary looking dude in a rain poncho (he was scary for two reasons: it wasn't raining and I don't think he had anything on *under* that poncho) broke out into this Martha Graham style dance routine.

And the whole time he's playing the stranger who abducted my guitar is grinning at me.

He stopped playing with a flourish. "Now, that ain't nothing. Nothing! Put a guitar like this in the right hands and then you'd have something. I can pick a little blues now but you, well I don't know what you were doing."

"That's what my dad says. He comes out when I practice and says, 'that ain't the blues, that's crap.' And goes back inside."

"Your daddy is a smart man."

He handed my guitar back to me. " Make an E chord . . . ok, now we know that you're smart enough to know what an E chord is. Now I'm gonna show you something. Gonna show you how to bounce that E chord. You put that bounce into that E chord and you'll have something.

You've got to bounce it, son. You put some bounce in that chord and even though you can't play the blues these folks won't ever know the difference."

"Why do I have to bounce it?"

"Because you can't play the guitar! Now do like I tell you, give me some bass. I said give me some *bass*, son! Hit that thing like you mean it. You're acting like you're afraid of that guitar. It ain't going to do nothing you don't tell it to so *hit* that thing!"

We sat like that long enough for a few trains to go by. I couldn't play exactly what he was showing me yet (it took me a few years of concentrated effort to actually make it work) but I could see the logic of it. I had an idea that I might be able to become a half decent country blues guitar player after all.

Strike the bass and let it ring. Hammer on the full chord while the bass is ringing and while *that's* ringing hammer on an extra note in the chord. Dropping in the note to make it an E6 is cool.

An E7 isn't quite as cool but it will work in a pinch. Slide into the A and slide into the B. Go back and bounce the E again.

I had never heard a guitar played in this manner before and I have yet to run into anybody else who plays that way. It was a simple approach to the guitar in some respects because the melody line is dropped in almost as an afterthought. In other ways it was mind-bendingly complex because it took the rhythm and *did* things to it. Instead of a boom-chuck or a bump-dit it took basic patterns and twisted them into a running shuffle beat that to this day makes my heart beat faster.

This wasn't the blues or country guitar I used to hear white guys playing in coffee shops. This wasn't trying to copy a bunch of meaningless notes out of a book. This was *power*. Power of a kind that up until then I had only heard people talk about and pretend to understand. Power to make the bunch of stuffy looking office drones close their eyes and daydream about driving into the night in a '59 Caddy wearing Ray-Ban shades with an electric guitar on the rear seat, a blonde in the passenger seat and a bag of mojo hand in the glove box. Power to bring out the good inside of you with a cheer and bring out the bad in you with a scream.

I remember sitting there while that Philly subway station reek covered me like a wet towel. I held my guitar and thought that maybe, just maybe, this was the key that my father told me I needed to find before I could make any sense out of the guitar.

"This" I said to myself, "is the blues."

"What did you say?" He asked me. "Did I hear you say *blues*? Don't be saying that word around *me*! Maybe if you could do something but not yet, not now!"

"Ah, nothing. What am I supposed to do about this B chord?"

We sat there on that bench for a while longer in the funky stink of that subway station. People were stopping to watch us bicker at each other like we were putting on some kind of a show. Every time I started to acknowledge the crowd the old guy would yell at me to pay attention to *him*. He answered all of my questions by first swearing and then yelling at me that nothing mattered but the rhythm.

He was still cussing me as he got up to leave. I said I didn't know how to thank him. He took my cigarettes and the money from my guitar case, said that would do just fine and got on the train. He was cussing me the whole time. As the train pulled away it hit me that I had never gotten around to asking him his name.

I waved goodbye and wondered if I was going to have enough money to cover the fare to get back home.

My mother makes patchwork quilts. She takes these little bits and pieces of cloth and makes beautiful geometric patterns that come together one piece at a time. It always amazes me that something as useless as a handful of calico scraps can become something beautiful and useful when put together properly. That's a good analogy to keep in mind as you start heading out to pick because learning to play the banjo has a lot in common with one of my mothers' quilts. We don't learn from one source but rather a collection of chance encounters. After a while every song you play becomes a patchwork of ideas that you picked up along the way. Sometimes I'll be playing a song and it will hit me that in just that one tune I can see bits and pieces from almost every musician I've ever met.

A lot of the musicians who added a scrap or two to my patchwork fall into a category that I like to refer to as "the cool old dudes." I can't tell you how many times I've had some old guy who didn't look smart enough to find his way home grab my banjo or guitar and just, to use a phrase from the drag racers in Crisfield, take me to school.

They weren't always gentle. Sometimes they were pretty rough but they were almost always honest. When I got it right they'd say so. When I got it wrong they'd say so. There was one cool old dude I met years ago at a festival in Pennsylvania who informed me that I was playing "bad enough to hurt his feelings." After I managed to stop laughing he sat down for an hour and helped me work out some Mississippi John Hurt songs.

Wherever you live I promise you that there is more than one cool old dude in your neck of the woods. They are not always easy to find. In fact it almost seems that when you go out looking for them they go into hiding or something. But if you get in the habit of taking your banjo with you everywhere the cool old dude in your town will find you.

When the weather is warm move your daily practice routine out to the front porch. Get a gig bag with a shoulder strap and get used to keeping your banjo close at hand wherever you go. The first step is to get out and be seen *with* your banjo. Don't wait until you are "ready" or "good enough" because that never happens. You don't have the luxury of being overly self-conscious if you really want to learn your instrument. If all you can do is play three songs that's three more songs than most of the other people out there can play. Get out and, as Woody Guthrie once put it, "inject yourself into the bloodstream of the people."

I've jammed with cool old dudes in parking lots, libraries, grocery stores, shopping malls, doctor's offices, train stations and most anyplace else you might think of. If you just sort of wander around you'll hear some old guy say, "Hey, is that a banjo?" Things will take off from there.

There is an old saying that goes, "When the student is ready the master will appear." Get out there and be ready. Accept the criticism as graciously as you accept the help. Always offer to at least buy the cool old dude a cup of coffee and be sure to keep a couple of bucks in your sneaker for the fare home, just in case.

"I've always wanted to play the banjo!"

"You know, I've always wanted to play the banjo!"

I was trying to keep my dog from bolting off the exam table so I was able to chew on my reply for a second. I'd been taking my dog to this veterinarian's office for almost ten years and at some point in every visit he said the same thing: "You know, I've always wanted to play the banjo!"

I usually would reply with something like "well then you ought to go ahead and do it" and offer to loan him a banjo. I always knew he would come up with some kind of excuse so it was a safe thing to say.

Any other day I might have said the same thing but as much as I liked the guy the routine was starting to drive me half crazy. I mean ten years! That would drive a saint to sleeping in on Sunday.

So I told him to stop by the house, take home one of my extra banjos and Dear Old Dad and I would help him get started. If he didn't want to do that then stop telling me "You know, I've always wanted to play the banjo!" because it's been ten years and he's starting to drive me nuts.

A day or two later he was on my front porch with an expression on his face that I imagine old Harry Houdini must have had before he let himself be hung by his feet from a skyscraper for one of those straightjacket escapes. A look that says, "What the *heck* am I getting into?"

I loaned him one of our extra banjos and showed him some basic stuff. It was rough going at first because the guy wouldn't stop shaking. It was like he wanted to play the banjo so badly that it had him half terrified. I was reminded of how I felt when I first started.

He got through the first lesson and started coming around once in a while for some more pointers.

It took him a few weeks to lose that "What the *heck* am I getting into?" expression and quicker than a blink I had my old banjo back and he was playing his own banjo.

Over the next few months I could see his confidence building up. About a year or so later he came by with his first banjo student. He started talking about starting up a jam session and that the preacher at his church might play a little fiddle. The next thing I know we've got a small jam going once a month at his place. People are starting to show up wanting to learn the banjo or the guitar.

His first banjo student had the rather scary habit of not breathing whenever he tried to play in front of people. At one of the jams either my father or I made a crack about how he was going to wind up needing an iron lung if he kept holding his breath like that. His nickname from that moment on became Ironlung.

The fiddle-playing preacher showed up. Another guy came by and started working on the guitar. Things started to come together. The veterinarian who always wanted to play the banjo became a banjo teacher. It's funny to watch him now because even the way he holds his instrument has changed over the last couple of years.

Ironlung learned how to breathe and play at the same time and his wife decided to start playing the bass. She had him drive up to Pennsylvania to buy a bass fiddle and before I knew it she was playing with us at the jam.

Every time I talk to the guys I hear about somebody new coming to the jam. The group is making an effort to reach out to more people. They are also doing some community service stuff like playing at nursing homes.

It's amazing to me how many lives just loaning somebody a banjo can touch. What's even more amazing is how much I got back from the deal. The people coming to the jam have become part of my family. And while I might teach them a chord or a lick they have taught me a few things about stuff more important than music.

I mean just having a Baptist preacher at the jam was a real boost for my behavior modification skills.

The first few times he came to the session I was half terrified that I would either start swearing like a French Quarter concierge or, even worse, break out into a song like God Bless the Bastard King Of England or Barnacle Bill The Sailor.

Don't get me wrong. I was raised in a good home and I am capable of remembering my manners. It's just that with the cool old dudes I used to hang around with a line like "What the &#%$ was *that* supposed to be?" was acceptable behavior.

All joking aside, getting to know the fiddling preacher was a joy because just like the veterinarian, Ironlung, the guitar guy and the other folks at the jam these are *good people*. And they really have made some amazing progress in a short period of time.

A couple of months ago a few of the guys went out to a big music festival. As soon as they got home we got a call from the veterinarian. He was all wired because some cool old dude and taken them aside and shared some tricks and some music with the group.

Funny how history repeats itself, isn't it?

When word gets out in your neighborhood that you are playing the banjo people are going to come to you and say, "I've always wanted to play the banjo." Be aware that how you respond can have a surprisingly far-reaching impact on the world around you. Every action is going to cause a ripple like a stone tossed in a still pond.

Every person you teach is going to teach others. Every song or lick you share with somebody is going to wind up being played by an untold number of banjo pickers at some point down the road. I know it's hard to believe that interacting with a single person can have any kind of impact on the world around you but it can and it will.

By sharing your music with other people you will get a chance to see the whole deal from a new angle. I can't tell you how many times I've been sharing a lick or technique with someone and just had a batch of new ideas pop into my head. That makes teaching a blast because I get to rediscover the instrument over and over again.

So pick up an old Harmony or some other extra banjo and keep it around the house. That way you'll have something to loan out when somebody tells you "I've always wanted to play the banjo."

Plateaus & Ruts

At some point as you progress you are going to hit a spot where nothing seems to come easy. I've got a friend who started playing the banjo a few years ago and the first time he hit this point he called me at around ten o'clock at night carrying on about being stuck in a rut. He wanted to know what to do to get out of that rut.

My father and I usually refer to this as hitting a plateau.

Imagine riding a bicycle down a nice level road and all of a sudden coming up on a huge hill. The cycling jumps from easy to hard in a matter of moments.

It's just like that when you are learning the banjo. You'll be going along smooth and then you run into a lick, song or concept that makes you feel like all of your progress has stopped.

It's not just frustrating, it's maddening.

The good news is that if you keep going the road always levels out again. The bad news is that there is always another hill a little bit farther down the road.

I was recently talking to a buddy of mine who has been playing the banjo professionally longer than I've been alive. He said that he *loves* hitting that rough patch of road. I asked him what he meant by that and he said, "Because I know that after I get through it I'm going to be a better banjo player."

So don't panic when you run into a technique that gives you a hard time. Just relax and look at the problem objectively. Think of it like having a brick wall in your path. You can stand there and try to knock down that wall by beating your head against it (not something I would recommend) or you can look for a way under, around or over that brick wall.

In other words, don't get stuck thinking that there is only one solution for the problem. There are bushel baskets of answers out there. You just have to be willing to see them.

Tying up the cat

A long, long time ago there was a monastery in Japan. The abbot in charge of this monastery was having a problem holding evening prayers because an old alley cat who had made it's home in the garden outside of the temple would always run to the top of the garden wall, yowl at the top of it's lungs and distract everybody.

The abbot was a patient guy but after a couple of weeks his nerves got on edge and he ordered one of the novice monks to tie the cat up every day before evening prayers.

Now, if you've ever tried to get a cat to do *anything* you know that this was no easy task. It wound up that just about every novice monk in the monastery had to lend a hand in chasing down the cat and tying it up. Things must have been pretty dull because over the next few weeks this became the high point of everybody's day.

Obviously this was long before cable TV.

A few years later the abbot died. The cat was still around so they continued to tie it up every evening before prayers. When that cat eventually died no one could remember why anybody had ever started tying up a cat every evening. But hey, why break a tradition? A new cat was brought into the monastery and tied up every night.

Centuries later the members of the monastery were writing scholarly treatises about the religious significance of tying up a cat before evening prayers.

Now and then you are going to run into somebody who is going to tell you that you have to play a song in a certain key, a specific tuning or copy the exact arrangement of some other banjo player. If you ask this person why you have to do any of these things he will give you a horrified look and say, "Because it's traditional."

I'm not going to tell you what to do. That's up to you. But before you follow blindly along stop and ask yourself if this person isn't asking you to tie up a cat.

Hidden Potential

"Isn't it *beautiful*? When I'm done fixing her up it's going to be *fine!*"

The object of my friend's affection was lying on the counter of the guitar shop. I am not often left speechless by anything. Looking at this guitar and listening to my buddy talk about fixing it had done just that; left me utterly speechless.

It was a guitar. A big guitar. That was all I could tell by looking at it because the whole thing had been smothered with bright green metal flake automotive paint. The wack-job who had painted the guitar had apparently been proud enough of his work to sign the canvas because the word "Mark" was scribbled across the front of the guitar with bright *yellow* metal flake auto paint.

It was also pretty banged up. There was a sunken spot by the bridge that looked to me like something nasty was going on with the bracing that held the guitar together. The pick-guard was a homemade affair that looked suspiciously like a kitchen countertop. There was a crack across the top running under the pick-guard so I figured at some point somebody was doing a bit of home repair. The only thing that hadn't been mangled on this guitar was the name on the headstock. Sitting like a cherry on a chicken manure sundae was a gold decal proclaiming that at some point in the past this had once been a Gibson guitar.

At the moment it looked like a sunflower that had just been run over by a tractor. A surrealist vision of what a country guitar should be. It looked like something from a yard sale in Ethiopia.

It looked like trouble.

I stood there trying to think of something to say. I mean, he wasn't asking for my advice. He had already decided that he was going buy the thing. I didn't know what he was going to *do* with it because there was no way this thing would ever play.

But he was my friend. You don't knock your friends dreams. So I did what friends usually do when they are faced with a situation like this. I just shrugged and said, "It's a guitar all right."

"Oh come on," he said, "It's beautiful! When I get her fixed up it's going to be really great. You'll see. She's going to *ring!*"

I just chewed on the inside of my check and said, "It's a guitar all right."

He bought the guitar. The guy behind the counter was so shocked that somebody wanted to actually buy the beastly thing that he never thought to stick it to my buddy on the price. I'm sure he spent a few sleepless nights later on wondering just how much my friend really would have been willing to pay for the used-to-be-a-Gibson.

On the way home he told me that he wanted to get some paint stripper. The first step was going to have to be getting that paint off the guitar. I stopped at a Wal-Mart and sprung for a couple of bottles of the weakest paint stripper I could find. I figured it was the least I could do. You always support your friends, even when they want to buy a mongrel Gibson.

I dropped him off at his house and tried to forget about the guitar. A few days later he called me and asked me what I knew about fixing guitars.

"What's wrong, was the top crack pretty bad?" I asked him.

"Oh, I'm not worried about *that*! I've got Popsicle sticks for that." He said, "I just can't remember how the pieces go back together."

"Pieces?" I was having a hard time getting this. "What do you mean Pieces?"

He started to laugh. "Oh! I didn't tell you that the stuff you got me, the paint stripper? Well it was too slow so I got a bucket of that stuff they use at the boat yard . . ."

I was horrified. "You mean marine stripper? That stuff will eat through everything!"

"Oh yeah its great!" He said. "I smeared that stuff all over the guitar and that paint just came off in sheets! Then it ate through the glue and the binding started to dissolve. I had to open all of the windows in the house because the fumes go so bad . . ."

"I'll be right over." I said. "I've got to see this."

So I drove over to his house to see the guitar. There were a couple of pieces over here and a couple of pieces over there. And my friend is telling me "everything is going according to plan."

Over the next few months I would get a call about once a week from my friend with a progress report on what my father and I had started to call 'The Guitar of Doom'.

I don't want to think about how many hours he spent sanding down every bit of wood and gluing it back into place. He repaired the cracks in the top with Popsicle sticks and replaced all of the binding that the marine stripper had dissolved. It took him a week or two to figure out how to glue the binding in place and I don't know what kind of glue he used to put all of the wood back together.

After a while I got a call and my friend told me that it was finished. He wanted me to be there when he strung it up for the first time.

When I got to his place and saw the guitar I didn't know what to think. I'd seen some ugly things in my time, but this, this was a piece of work.

The green paint was all gone but the bare wood was stained in a variety of ways. The cracks were all repaired from the back but the top of the guitar was still covered with scars. If Frankenstein played the guitar it would have looked like this.

The first thing he asked me when he handed it to me was "Isn't it beautiful?"

I just nodded and said, "It's a guitar."

So we sat in his living room and strung up the guitar. He handed it to me and asked me to tune it up. I wasn't thrilled with the idea. It would have been just my luck to have the thing collapse like an old outhouse in a windstorm as soon as I got it up to concert pitch but I accepted the job as graciously as I could.

As I got the first string up around E I had to cock my head a little bit in surprise. Not because it was holding together. It was because I was starting to hear something. By the time I got the sixth string in tune I was looking back and forth between the guitar and my friend. "Do you hear that?" I asked him.

"Oh yeah." He said. "Sweet isn't she?"

I didn't answer right away. Once I had it in tune I ran a couple of chords and then went into a fingerstyle arrangement of *Freight Train*. After a couple of times through I just stopped and stared at my friend.

This guitar. This ugly, dog-eared box of splinters that shouldn't even hold together under the strain of concert tuning wasn't just loud. It was alive. In all of my years of playing I've never picked up a guitar like this. It was a cannon. It was the loudest and most powerful flattop box I have ever played.

My friend just grinned at me and said "And you thought I was either crazy or stupid!"

"I still do." I said "But this is a *nice* guitar!"

Sometimes lessons pop up in the most unlikely places. Sometimes you can learn more from being proven wrong than from being proven right.

I never got over how powerful that guitar turned out to be. It was as ugly as homemade soap but there was something special about it. I didn't see the potential in that old guitar but my friend did. He looked beyond the green paint and the cracks in the top and saw what was really there. He was also willing to put in a lot of hours chipping away at the rough edges.

When you go out to jams you may run into somebody with a mongrel guitar or banjo. Be sure to look at what's really there before you pass it off. You might be pleasantly surprised at what you find.

The chicken dancers

There is a really weird sociological phenomenon that happens when people hear a banjo.

It is often referred to as "the chicken dance" by banjo players around the world.

You will be playing somewhere and people will all of a sudden jump up, tuck in their arms, start bobbing their heads and make these odd hopping motions while flapping their elbows up and down.

I don't know why people do this. I know of some banjo players that have driven themselves half-crazy (not too much of a jump for most of us) trying to figure out why the chicken dance happens.

It's going to happen to you. Just about anywhere you go to play the banjo somebody is going to be inspired to break out in a chicken dance. And these chickens usually travel in flocks. I've seen whole crowds of people jump up and start flapping.

How you handle it is up to you. My advice would be to just go along with it. Even if they are acting like idiots they are reacting to your music in a way that doesn't involve throwing things at you.

Don't quit your day job

A rainstorm always looks different when you are flat on your back in a mud puddle.

I managed to tune out my dad's mix of cursing and questioning for a few moments and decided to have a little chat with God.

"So boss, um. I mean 'Boss.' Is this one of those little life lesson deals?"

There wasn't any answer. Unless I decided to take the fact that it started raining even harder as some kind of metaphysical yes or no.

I figured I would ponder on that for a little while. I didn't really want to get up. Somewhere between nearly getting heat stroke, nearly having to gnaw my finger off like a weasel in a trap and getting hit by lighting I had reached a point where just dragging myself out of this mud puddle was going to take a minor miracle.

I guess I should explain what had happened.

My father and I were in Pennsylvania to do a show in this neat old vaudeville era theater. As soon as we got to the place we just knew, I mean we just *knew* things were going to go wrong. Sort of the way you can sometimes smell a thunderstorm right before it hits.

It started when we were doing the sound check. The theater had an old air conditioning system that blew the cold air from massive grates on either side of the stage. As we were setting up the microphones a horrible clanking noise started pounding out of the grates and the cold air changed to cool.

Then it started blowing warm air.

And then it stopped blowing altogether.

I guess it wouldn't have been that big of a deal if we weren't in the middle of a record-breaking heat wave. It was the hottest day anybody could remember in the great state of Pennsylvania.

If you have never been on stage you can't know just how warm it can get under the lights. Take a hot day in a big old theater with no air-conditioning and things get really hot.

Everybody else involved with the show that night said to heck with it. Cancel the show. Let's all go home. But the guy who owned the theater said that people had already bought tickets. They were already in the lobby waiting for a show. Was he supposed to refund the money and send them home?

I looked at Dad. Dad looked at me. We had a silent conversation across the room. The show goes on. It's the right thing to do.

So the folks who had made the trip and were willing to sit in the heat and watch a couple of bozos from Maryland sing and play the banjo got their show.

To say that it was hot under those lights is putting it mildly. I was sweating so badly that it was hard to fret my banjo strings. I'd push down on the frets and my fingers would just slide around. The sweat was pouring in my eyes and I couldn't stop playing to bring my hand up to my face and clear them. It was like performing on the surface of the sun. I kept waiting for camels to start pacing around on the stage.

But we did it. The people in the audience were happy. The fellow who ran the theater was as happy as a guy with a busted high-dollar air-conditioning system in a funky old theater can be. We were happy that we had seen the job through and even happier that it was over.

We skipped the after-show kissing hands and shaking babies routine and headed right back to our trailer. We just wanted to get to the campground and cool down for a while.

When we got to our trailer I decided to start getting it ready so that we could leave bright and early in the morning

The trailer had this awning on one side of it. I hit the latches and gave the rope a tug to free up the springs that would roll the awning up. I was still all sweaty and tired so I really wasn't paying attention to what I was doing. The awning snapped up into the side of the trailer and rolled my index finger right up with it.

It was almost too much to believe. One second I'm on the ground holding the rope and the next thing I know I'm hanging up in the air by my finger.

I did what any rational person does in a situation like this. I screamed my head off.

To make things even more interesting, as if they hadn't been interesting enough up to that point, I was hanging right in front of the trailer door. Dad was in the trailer and when he heard me screaming he ran to the door and threw it open to see what was going on.

Well he *tried* to throw open the door. All he really managed to do was hit me with the door. That hurt but it also started me swinging by my rolled up finger and that *really* hurt.

So I'm hanging there yelling my head off and my father is banging me with the door and yelling his head off when the skies opened up and the rain came down in buckets.

Now in most emergency situations my father can keep perfectly calm and remain in control. But when it comes to an emergency involving me he has this unusual habit of telling me what a jackass I am for getting into trouble. I guess he thinks it helps in some way. Well he couldn't push the door open enough to *help* me but he *could* push the door open enough to yell at me.

So he's yelling. I'm yelling. It was pouring down rain and I'm caught like a rat in a trap.

"How are you going to get out of this mess you idiot?" Dad asked me.

"Well it would help if you would stop hitting me with the freaking door!" I yelled at him.

After a few tries I managed to swing myself to one side far enough to pop the spring latch that was keeping the awning up in spite of my weight. I managed to get my feet pressed on the side of the trailer for leverage and hit the ground like a ton of bricks when I pulled my hand free.

I managed to crawl into the trailer out of the rain. Pop asked me if I was all right and then promptly went back to telling me what an idiot I am and asking how on earth somebody could maim themselves rolling up an awing.

"Gee and a little while ago I was saying to myself that this day couldn't get any worse!" I said.

"Trust me son, it can always get worse." He said "I'm going to go out and hook the trailer to the truck so we can leave in the morning."

"I'll do it, pop. I'm already soaked." I said.

"Sure you don't want to rest up your finger?" he asked me.

I didn't bother to reply. I just headed back out into the rain.

I had a devil of a time getting the trailer ready to hook up. The first time I tried to back the truck up I got everything messed up so I went back around to jack the front end of the trailer up again.

Except this time I didn't bother to put the old piece of board down that we usually use under the jack. I just let it sink a little bit in the mud. I mean, what was going to happen?

As I'm standing there with both hands on the jack something did happen. I heard this funny kind of sizzle followed right away by a loud pop. The next thing I knew the trailer was getting smaller.

At least that's how it seemed at first. Then it occurred to me that the trailer wasn't getting smaller I was just flying backwards through the air.

I was still marveling at the way perspective can trick you like that when I hit the ground. Then I wasn't looking at the trailer anymore. I was looking at the sky.

Later on as we were driving home we debated whether or not I had been hit by lightning. It's the only answer we could ever come up with. We drove home through the rain and pop said that if we couldn't make any money playing the banjo we could always go on the road as a traveling stunt show. We laughed all the way back to Maryland.

Trust me my friends. Gigs will go bad once in a while. Things will go the exact opposite of how you plan them. It comes with the territory. I think there is a lot of truth to the old saying that musicians don't work for the money; they just do it for the stories they can tell down the road.

When things go wrong keep your cool. Roll with the punches.

And be careful around awnings.

Stage Fright

"What do you want, kid?" The guy running the open stage at the festival asked me.

"My dad and me, we're big time banjo players from Nashville." I said. "We're on our way home from a gag and thought we'd play for the folks."

One of the old guitar pickers hanging out backstage broke out laughing. The guy running things just gave me a puzzled look.

"You mean a gig, don't you?" He asked me.

"Umm . . . we call them gags now, sir." I said. " Maybe you ought to keep up with the lingo."

This was too much for the old guys who had gathered around. They were laughing so hard they were doubled over and tears were streaming from their eyes.

I did my best to play it cool. The truth was this was only the second festival I had ever been to in my life. I didn't know more than about three and a half songs and my father had no idea that I was volunteering us to perform on stage.

The guy running things was kind of angry that I was wasting his time. He started to tell me to get lost but one of the old guys said "Put the kid on. He's got guts."

A couple more of them started telling him to put me on the stage so the guy shook his head and said, "You're on in fifteen minutes."

My heart started beating faster. Fifteen minutes? I started to ask for more time to get ready but one of the old guys cuffed me on the back of the head and said, "Don't push your luck. Go get your daddy, get on the stage and do your best."

The look on my father's face when I told him we were going on stage in a few minutes was priceless. "Are you out of your mind? You don't even know any songs!"

"Well I know three. Actually, two songs and half of one. We can play those." I said.

I have to give my dad credit. He was as terrified as I was but he went along with me. "Yeah. Let's do it." He said.

So we went out on a flatbed trailer that had been converted into a stage for the festival. I was so scared that I couldn't stop shaking and when I looked out at the crowd and saw three thousand people looking at me I started shaking harder.

I glanced over to my dad who was shaking every bit as much as I was and he gave me a thumbs up sign. I gave a quick look the other way and one of the old guys from backstage gave me another thumbs up sign. I looked out in the crowd and spotted my grandfather who didn't give me a thumbs up sign because he was too busy laughing at me.

Dad told the audience about how I had shanghaied him into getting on stage. Everybody got a good laugh at that. We played and sang the first of our two and a half songs and the crowd just went crazy. Pop started to relax and that helped me to relax. We went into our next song and people were clapping along. Other people who were on the edge of the field started to come a little bit closer to the stage. It hit me right about then that the crowd was enjoying us. This was kind of puzzling to me because I was pretty sure that we really stank. We finished our set (I just faked the other half of the third song) and everybody started applauding us. I'm grinning at dad and dad is grinning back at me. I think we both felt like we were on top of the world right about then.

When we climbed off the stage there was a gang of other musicians waiting for us wanting to know just *where* we had learned to play the banjo that way. The old guys were patting me on the back saying "Good job!" and I'm trying to figure out why everybody was all happy for us. I mean we only knew two and a half songs.

I walked over to the old guy who had told me not to push my luck. "That was pretty awful, kid. Matter of fact it stank." He said.

"That's what I thought,"

"Yeah, But you did it. And that took a lot of nerve."

"Thanks."

"It gets easier," He said. "Come back next year and do better. You're part of the thing now." And he walked away.

Brain freeze

When an archer is shooting for nothing, he has all his skill.
If he shoots for a brass buckle, he is already nervous.
If he shoots for a prize of gold, he goes blind or sees two targets -
he is out of his mind!

His skill has not changed. But the prize divides him.
He cares. He thinks more of winning than of shooting-
and the need to win drains him of power.
-Chuang Tzu

I always have somebody asking me about brain-freeze.

You know what I mean. You go somewhere with your banjo and you really want to show off and impress the heck out of everybody but when you go to hit a string everything goes wrong. And the more you want to impress the audience the worse you wind up playing.

Or just as frustrating, you set a goal and focus on it, like playing a song note-for-note from a recording. You run through the song over and over again trying to make sure that every note is perfect but it seems like every time that you play the song your playing takes a step backwards instead of forwards.

I could think up many pages of scenarios like this but in the end it all boils down to being focused on *you* instead of the music.

A lot of beginning banjo pickers fret almost nonstop about what people will think about them, their playing, the brand of banjo they play (as if the name on the headstock makes any difference) and so much other "stuff" that they wind up working against themselves. Instead of flowing with the music they wind up fighting against it. Instead of practicing because it's fun to kick back for an hour with a banjo they practice to get everything perfect.

It might be good to reorganize your priorities in this department now because if you want to entertain people, play in a band or even just sit in with the house band for a square dance you won't cut the mustard if you think it's all about *you*.

In a band you have to be doing your best to support your fellow musicians. If you are performing solo for an audience you have to be aware of what the people in the audience want to hear. At a dance you have to think about laying down a solid rhythm for the dancers.

In all of those situations nobody is going to care if you can play all of the songs on the *Foggy Mountain Banjo* album. Nobody is going to care if you are in double-augmented-something-or-another tuning. They just want you to do your job.

If you can grasp this you can realize that it's ok to make a mistake. You must remember that people want to hear *you* play the banjo.
A note for note rendition of some other famous banjo player's music is not you! If you can accept the fact that you are who you are and just play because you want to share this really neat instrument you'll find that things start to get easier.

In fact if you stop thinking about what you are doing there won't be any fussing or fidgeting around before you play a song. You'll just do it. It's not a hard thing to do but at the same time it is. You just have to stop worrying about **you**.

A good way to get started on this is to share yourself with your community. Take your banjo to the local nursing home and play for the folks there. Talk to them and learn some of the songs they want to hear. Give free banjo lessons on your front porch. Fix up a couple of old banjos and loan them out to people. Play for tips down at the subway station and give the money to charity.

Just start working to make a difference in the world around you. You don't have to go crazy like old man Scrooge on Christmas morning. Just act whenever you see a need that you can fill. Even if you can't play that well yet you can still give of your time.

I know it sounds crazy but the less you think about yourself the more people will think of you and the music that you make.

One of the old timers

It was one of those picture-postcard perfect Pennsylvania August days. The kind of day where any problems you might have on your mind just sort of fade away in the heat while the breeze coming through the forest runs across your brow so cool and soft that you can't help but give a little sigh.

I was on the edge of the woods that surround the park with my father. The field where I had wandered so long ago with a banjo that I didn't quite know how to play was lying wide open to the sun. Every corner of the place was filled with the sent of fresh cut grass.

It was good to be back but it was also a little bittersweet because the old man with the cigar and his buddies were nowhere to be found. I had gotten word over the years that most of them had passed on and the few that were left were too old and too sick to go out and pick.

The weird thing about it all was I realized right about then how much I had changed. Shoot, how both of us had changed. Since coming to this festival for the first time my father and I had performed on stages on both sides of the Mississippi. The two of us had come a long, long way together from wandering around hoping somebody would take the time to share a lick or a trick with us to becoming seasoned performers. We had seen things and done things that we never would have dreamed we were capable of back when we first came here.

Some friends of ours turned up after a while. An old banjo-picking buddy who we hadn't seen in years wandered over. By some miracle my grandfather had convinced one of my uncles to load up the wheelchair and come out to the park. We spent that perfect August afternoon picking and singing in the shade not knowing that it was the last time we would all be together like this.

A crowd started to gather around. A big one. The kind of crowd I used to see around the old timers when they were jamming here years ago. I kept looking over at my father and he kept looking over at me wondering just what was happening.

Folks started to sing along and people started to drag out instruments and play along. Between songs something kind of strange started happening. I was getting requests for help. Kids were creeping up fighting their shyness to see my guitar or get a closer look at my banjo. A lot of them were looking at me like I was some kind of an old timer.

"Hey, do you think you could help me tune my guitar?"

"Can you show me how to make an E chord on my banjo?"

"Can you help me with this guitar strap?"

"Can you help me with . . ."

Just for a moment I would have sworn that I heard that cigar chewing old man laugh but it might have been my dad. He had already picked up on what was happening and was getting a pretty good chuckle out of it all. He knew what I was going to say to them.

I stuck a cigarette in the corner of my mouth, crossed my arms over my guitar and turned to the people around me.

"All right" I said to them, "show me what you've got."

Get lost

This is the part where I say to you "Get lost. Go on and work on that. Don't come back until you can do like we showed you."

There is more I'd like to share with you. There are more songs, more techniques and more stories. In the end there is always more to learn. That's the amazing thing about music. It's a path that just keeps going.

I wish you the best. I hope the banjo brings great joy to your life and the lives of the people around you. I hope you are never embarrassed to sing. I hope you are never afraid to try. I hope that you manage to ignore the people who say it can't be done.

Remember to look around you. If you see a need fill it. Always be willing to make time to show somebody a lick or two. When you have a bad day make a donation to charity in the name of somebody you really don't like. Be the change you want to see in the world.

And never step in anything soft.